TO MOM & DAD, MY BIGGEST FANS FROM DAY ONE.
AND TO MY READERS, YOU MADE THIS POSSIBLE.

PAGE STREET
PUBLISHING CO.

First published in 2017 by
Page Street Publishing Co.
27 Congress Street, Suite 105
Salem, MA 01970
www.pagestreetpublishing.com

Distributed by Macmillan, sales in Canada by The Canadian Manda Group.

20   19   18   17   1   2   3   4

ISBN-13: 978-1-62414-333-5
ISBN-10: 1-62414-333-4

Library of Congress Control Number: 2016949512

Cover and book design by Page Street Publishing Co.
Photography by Amanda Drozdz

Printed and bound in China

Page Street is proud to be a member of 1% for the Planet. Members donate one percent of their sales to one or more of the over 1,500 environmental and sustainability charities across the globe who participate in this program.

Contents

Coffeehouse Favorites

FOR THOSE MOMENTS WHEN ONLY A LITTLE SOMETHING EXTRA WILL DO

Chocolate Lovers' Muffins

THE HEALTHY ANSWER TO THOSE COCOA CRAVINGS

Single-Serve Minute Muffins 109

BECAUSE SOMETIMES YOU JUST NEED A SINGLE MUFFIN IN LESS THAN 5 MINUTES

Healthy Brownies and Snack Bars 135

MUFFINS' CHEWIER, FUDGIER AND MORE RECTANGULAR COUSINS

Soft & Chewy Flourless Cookies   159

THE COOKIES YOU KNOW AND LOVE—MINUS THE FLOUR

Introduction

I have a passion for healthy living, and I really love showing people how they can use food to look and feel their best. From a young age, my mom taught me that food is medicine and that the things we put in our bodies have a huge impact on how we feel. Her home-cooked meals and freshly baked treats instilled in me not only a love for working in the kitchen with real food, but for getting creative and finding healthier ways to satisfy my massive sweet tooth.

Yup, I have one of those. It's been with me for as long as I can remember, and it means that you'll never find me passing on dessert or going a day without a sweet treat. That's actually another important life lesson my mom taught me—that restriction gets you nowhere. Never once do I remember her being an advocate for deprivation. She simply told me to enjoy my sweet treats but "make smarter choices," which is an approach I've adopted into all of the recipe development I do now and how I manage to satisfy my sweet tooth while living a healthy lifestyle.

All of the muffins, brownies, bars and cookies you'll find in this book make a smart choice. Each one is flourless and is either made with 100 percent whole grain oats or is completely grain-free. They're much lower in sugar than traditional desserts and rely on natural sweeteners like honey, maple syrup or coconut palm sugar for their sweetness. They also taste straight up delicious and don't make you feel like you're making any sacrifices while following a healthy diet.

I've made these recipes as real life–friendly as possible, meaning that they're all quick and easy to prepare and use ingredients that you probably keep stocked in your kitchen. It's my hope that you'll be able to adopt them into your daily life and use them to help you look and feel your best . . . so let's dive right in!

Love,

Amanda

NOTE

Before you get started, here's a quick tip. Since many of these recipes are oil-free, they have a tendency to stick to standard baking paper liners. I recommend using parchment paper baking liners for best results and no sticking! Alternatively, you can use no liners and simply grease the cups of your baking pan with baking spray.

Classic Favorites

We all have a favorite muffin—a particular flavor that holds
a special place in our hearts. For some it might be simple
Chocolate Chip Muffins (page 11); for others, it might be
bright and fresh Lemon Poppy Seed Muffins (page 31).
For this chapter, I've chosen 14 classic flavors that we all know
and love. They're the simple and comforting muffins that we
grew up on, only this time with a healthier twist. Each one of
these muffins is made without flour, oil or refined sugar, but
they come out so soft, tender and flavorful that you'd never
be able to tell. They're a perfect treat for those looking for
something that's both healthy and delicious; they're
for anyone who loves muffins, really.

Chocolate Chip Muffins

GLUTEN-FREE, OIL-FREE, DAIRY-FREE OPTION*

This particular muffin holds a special place in my heart because it's based on the very first flourless muffin recipe I ever created. This new and improved version is just as healthy and made without any flour, butter or oil, but it now has a fluffier texture that makes it even harder to differentiate from a traditional muffin.

YIELD: 10-12 MUFFINS

1¼ cup (101 g) rolled oats (quick or old-fashioned)

3 tbsp (21 g) ground flaxseed

2 tsp (8 g) baking powder

¾ tsp baking soda

¼ tsp salt

3 large eggs

¼ cup (59 ml) unsweetened almond milk

6 tbsp (96 g) almond butter

6 tbsp (128 g) honey

1 tbsp (15 ml) vanilla extract

½ cup (90 g) semisweet chocolate chips (*for dairy-free, use vegan chocolate chips)

Preheat your oven to 350°F (177°C) and prepare a muffin pan by lining the cavities with parchment paper liners. Set aside.

Add the oats, ground flaxseed, baking powder, baking soda and salt to a high-speed blender. Process the ingredients on high until the oats have broken down into the consistency of a fine flour, about 10 seconds.

Add all of the remaining ingredients except for the chocolate chips. Process the ingredients on high until the batter becomes smooth and creamy, about 30 seconds. Periodically stop and scrape down the sides of your blender, if necessary. Finally, stir in the chocolate chips by hand.

Spoon the batter into the prepared muffin cups, filling each one about ¾ of the way full. Sprinkle the tops with additional chocolate chips, if desired.

Bake for 15–18 minutes, until the tops of your muffins begin to turn golden brown and a toothpick inserted into the center comes out clean. Allow the muffins to cool in the pan for 10 minutes before transferring them to a wire rack to cool completely. As soon as they've cooled, transfer them to an airtight container and store them at room temperature for up to 5 days, or freeze for up to 3 months.

Double Chocolate Muffins

GLUTEN–FREE, GRAIN–FREE, OIL–FREE, DAIRY–FREE OPTION*

Chocolate lovers rejoice! These soft and fudgy muffins pack a serious chocolate punch that's guaranteed to satisfy even the biggest cocoa craving. And the best part is that you can totally fit them into your healthy diet! Because they're 100 percent grain-free and rely on cocoa powder as the main dry ingredient, be sure to use a good quality, natural cocoa powder for the best results. To intensify the chocolate flavor even further, replace the semisweet chips with dark chocolate chunks.

YIELD: 10–12 MUFFINS

½ cup + 2 tbsp (50 g) unsweetened cocoa powder

3 tbsp (21 g) ground flaxseed

2 tsp (8 g) baking powder

1 tsp baking soda

¼ tsp salt

3 large eggs

⅓ cup (78 ml) unsweetened almond milk

6 tbsp (96 g) almond butter

½ cup (170 g) honey

1 tbsp (15 ml) vanilla extract

½ cup (90 g) semisweet chocolate chips (*for dairy-free, use vegan chocolate chips)

Preheat your oven to 350°F (177°C) and prepare a muffin pan by lining the cavities with parchment paper liners. Set aside.

Add the cocoa, ground flaxseed, baking powder, baking soda and salt to a high-speed blender and pulse a few times until all the dry ingredients become well combined.

Add all of the remaining ingredients except for the chocolate chips. Process the ingredients on high until the batter becomes smooth and creamy, about 30 seconds. Periodically stop and scrape down the sides of your blender, if necessary. Finally, stir in the chocolate chips by hand.

Spoon the batter into the prepared muffin cups, filling each one about ¾ of the way full. Sprinkle the tops with additional chocolate chips, if desired.

Bake for 20–22 minutes, until a toothpick inserted into the center comes out clean. Allow the muffins to cool in the pan for 10 minutes before transferring them to a wire rack to cool completely. As soon as they've cooled, transfer them to an airtight container and store them at room temperature for up to 5 days, or freeze for up to 3 months.

Blueberry Muffins

GLUTEN—FREE, OIL—FREE, DAIRY—FREE, REFINED SUGAR—FREE

Blueberries are one of those fruits that I could literally eat by the pound, especially in the summer months when they're fresh and extra sweet. I've paired them with a hefty dose of vanilla in these light and fluffy muffins, which means that every bite is loaded with flavor and berry-powered antioxidants.

YIELD: 10–12 MUFFINS

1¼ cups (101 g) rolled oats (quick or old-fashioned)

3 tbsp (21 g) ground flaxseed

2 tsp (8 g) baking powder

¾ tsp baking soda

¼ tsp salt

3 large eggs

¼ cup (59 ml) unsweetened almond milk

6 tbsp (96 g) almond butter

6 tbsp (128 g) honey

1 tbsp (15 ml) vanilla extract

¾ cup (105 g) blueberries, fresh or frozen

1 tbsp (7 g) coconut flour

Preheat your oven to 350°F (177°C) and prepare a muffin pan by lining the cavities with parchment paper liners. Set aside.

Add the oats, ground flaxseed, baking powder, baking soda and salt to a high-speed blender and process on high for about 10 seconds or until the oats have broken down into the consistency of a fine flour.

Add all of the remaining ingredients except for the blueberries and coconut flour, and process on high for about 30 seconds or until the batter becomes smooth and creamy. Periodically stop and scrape down the sides of your blender, if necessary.

Transfer the batter to a medium-sized mixing bowl (this makes it easier to prevent the berries from bleeding). Toss the blueberries in the 1 tablespoon (7 g) of coconut flour to prevent them from bleeding or sinking to the bottom of the muffins, and gently fold them into the batter.

Spoon the batter into the prepared muffin cups, filling each one about ¾ of the way full.

Bake for 15–18 minutes, until the tops of your muffins begin to turn golden brown and a toothpick inserted into the center comes out clean. Allow the muffins to cool in the pan for 10 minutes before transferring them to a wire rack to cool completely. As soon as they've cooled, transfer them to an airtight container and store them at room temperature for up to 5 days, or freeze for up to 3 months.

Banana Bread Muffins

GLUTEN-FREE, OIL-FREE, DAIRY-FREE, REFINED SUGAR-FREE

Say hello to the perfect way to use up those overripe bananas! Not only do these soft and fluffy muffins allow you to enjoy the comforting flavor of traditional banana bread, but also they come together in a fraction of the time compared to the classic quick bread. You definitely won't miss the flour, oil or refined sugar in these healthier muffins!

YIELD: 10–12 MUFFINS

1½ cups (121 g) rolled oats (quick or old-fashioned)

3 tbsp (21 g) ground flaxseed

1 tsp ground cinnamon

¼ tsp ground nutmeg

2 tsp (8 g) baking powder

¾ tsp baking soda

½ tsp salt

2 large eggs

½ cup (118 ml) unsweetened almond milk

¼ cup (64 g) almond butter

¼ cup (85 g) honey

2 tsp (10 ml) vanilla extract

2 medium-sized ripe bananas, mashed (about 1 cup [200 g])

Preheat your oven to 350°F (177°C) and prepare a muffin pan by lining the cavities with parchment paper liners. Set aside.

Add the oats, ground flaxseed, cinnamon, nutmeg, baking powder, baking soda and salt to a high-speed blender and process on high for about 10 seconds or until the oats have broken down into the consistency of a fine flour.

Add all of the remaining ingredients except for the mashed bananas and process on high for about 30 seconds or until the batter becomes smooth and creamy. Periodically stop and scrape down the sides of your blender, if necessary. Finally, fold in the mashed bananas by hand.

Spoon the batter into the prepared muffin cups, filling each one about ¾ of the way full.

Bake for 17–19 minutes, until the tops of your muffins begin to turn golden brown and a toothpick inserted into the center comes out clean. Allow the muffins to cool in the pan for 10 minutes before transferring them to a wire rack to cool completely. As soon as they've cooled, transfer them to an airtight container and store them at room temperature for up to 5 days, or freeze for up to 3 months.

Apple Cinnamon Muffins

GLUTEN-FREE, OIL-FREE, DAIRY-FREE, REFINED SUGAR-FREE

These soft and flavorful muffins stay extra moist thanks to a double dose of juicy apples. I've used Gala, Ambrosia and Pink Ladies while testing these, but try experimenting with different apple varieties to see which one you enjoy the most. You can also add in ½ cup (80 g) of raisins for a little bit of extra flavor and natural sweetness.

YIELD: 10–12 MUFFINS

1½ cups (121 g) rolled oats (quick or old-fashioned)

3 tbsp (21 g) ground flaxseed

2 tsp (5 g) ground cinnamon

¼ tsp ground nutmeg

2 tsp (8 g) baking powder

1 tsp baking soda

½ tsp salt

3 large eggs

½ cup (118 ml) unsweetened applesauce

6 tbsp (96 g) almond butter

6 tbsp (128 g) honey

1 tsp vanilla extract

1 cup (115 g) shredded apple, lightly squeezed of excess juice

Preheat your oven to 350°F (177°C) and prepare a muffin pan by lining the cavities with parchment paper liners. Set aside.

Add the oats, ground flaxseed, cinnamon, nutmeg, baking powder, baking soda and salt to a high-speed blender and process on high for about 10 seconds or until the oats have broken down into the consistency of a fine flour.

Add all of the remaining ingredients except for the apple, and process on high for about 30 seconds or until the batter becomes smooth and creamy. Periodically stop and scrape down the sides of your blender, if necessary. Finally, fold in the shredded apple by hand.

Spoon the batter into the prepared muffin cups, filling each one about ¾ of the way full.

Bake for 15–18 minutes, until the tops of your muffins begin to turn golden brown and a toothpick inserted into the center comes out clean. Allow the muffins to cool in the pan for 10 minutes before transferring them to a wire rack to cool completely. As soon as they've cooled, transfer them to an airtight container and store them at room temperature for up to 5 days, or freeze for up to 3 months.

NOTE

I like to place a handful of shredded apple between two paper towels and lightly squeeze it over the sink. This drains it of just the right amount of juice to allow the muffins to cook properly.

Chocolate Chip Zucchini Muffins

GLUTEN-FREE, OIL-FREE, DAIRY-FREE OPTION*

If you would have told me even a handful of years ago that I'd love putting zucchini in my snacks, I would have laughed myself sick. But I'm literally eating my words because zucchini is a miracle worker! Not only does it keep baked goods extra moist without the addition of any extra fat, but it's also a great way to get those picky eaters to eat more veggies.

YIELD: 10-12 MUFFINS

1½ cups (121 g) rolled oats (quick or old-fashioned)

3 tbsp (21 g) ground flaxseed

2 tsp (8 g) baking powder

1 tsp baking soda

¼ tsp salt

3 large eggs

¼ cup (59 ml) unsweetened almond milk

6 tbsp (96 g) almond butter

6 tbsp (128 g) honey

1 tbsp (15 ml) vanilla extract

1 cup (115 g) shredded zucchini, squeezed of excess liquid

½ cup (90 g) semisweet chocolate chips (*for dairy-free, use vegan chocolate chips)

Preheat your oven to 350°F (177°C) and prepare a muffin pan by lining the cavities with parchment paper liners. Set aside.

Add the oats, ground flaxseed, baking powder, baking soda and salt to a high-speed blender, and process on high for about 10 seconds or until the oats have broken down into the consistency of a fine flour.

Add all of the remaining ingredients except for the zucchini and chocolate chips, and process on high for about 30 seconds or until the batter becomes smooth and creamy. Periodically stop and scrape down the sides of your blender, if necessary. Finally, fold in the zucchini and chocolate chips by hand.

Spoon the batter into the prepared muffin cups, filling each one about ¾ of the way full. Sprinkle the tops with additional chocolate chips, if desired.

Bake for 15-18 minutes, until the tops of your muffins begin to turn golden brown and a toothpick inserted into the center comes out clean. Allow the muffins to cool in the pan for 10 minutes before transferring them to a wire rack to cool completely. As soon as they've cooled, transfer them to an airtight container and store them at room temperature for up to 5 days, or freeze for up to 3 months.

NOTE

I like to place a handful of shredded zucchini between two paper towels and squeeze it over the sink. This drains it of just the right amount of liquid to allow the muffins to cook properly.

Oat Bran Muffins

GLUTEN-FREE, OIL-FREE, DAIRY-FREE, REFINED SUGAR-FREE

Oat bran is the outer layer of the oat grain that's usually discarded during the processing of rolled oats. It's extremely high in soluble fiber, and it makes a great replacement for wheat bran for those with gluten sensitivities. These healthy muffins are touched with a hint of molasses, which gives them an irresistibly hearty flavor and aroma.

YIELD: 10-12 MUFFINS

¾ cup (60 g) rolled oats (quick or old-fashioned)

3 tbsp (21 g) ground flaxseed

½ tsp ground cinnamon

2 tsp (8 g) baking powder

1 tsp baking soda

¼ tsp salt

3 large eggs

⅔ cup (156 ml) unsweetened almond milk

6 tbsp (96 g) almond butter

¼ cup (85 g) honey

2 tbsp (44 g) molasses

1 tsp vanilla extract

¾ cup (90 g) oat bran

½ cup (76 g) raisins, soaked in warm water for 10 minutes and patted dry

Preheat your oven to 350°F (177°C) and prepare a muffin pan by lining the cavities with parchment paper liners. Set aside.

Add the oats, ground flaxseed, cinnamon, baking powder, baking soda and salt to a high-speed blender, and process on high for about 10 seconds or until the oats have broken down into the consistency of a fine flour.

Add all of the remaining ingredients except for the oat bran and raisins, and process on high for about 30 seconds or until the batter becomes smooth and creamy. Periodically stop and scrape down the sides of your blender, if necessary. The batter will be somewhat thin and runny. This is normal—the oat bran will soak up a lot of the liquid and thicken the batter.

Transfer the batter to a medium-sized mixing bowl and fold in the oat bran and raisins by hand, mixing well to ensure that everything becomes fully incorporated. Let the batter sit for about 10 minutes to give the bran a chance to soften up and soak up some of the liquid.

Spoon the batter into the prepared muffin cups, filling each one about ¾ of the way full.

Bake for 17-19 minutes, until the tops of your muffins begin to turn golden brown and a toothpick inserted into the center comes out clean. Allow the muffins to cool in the pan for 10 minutes before transferring them to a wire rack to cool completely. As soon as they've cooled, transfer them to an airtight container and store them at room temperature for up to 5 days, or freeze for up to 3 months.

NOTE

If you don't have any molasses, you can substitute for it an additional 2 tablespoons (40 g) of honey instead, but the flavor of the finished product will be slightly different.

Banana Walnut Muffins

GLUTEN-FREE, OIL-FREE, DAIRY-FREE, REFINED SUGAR-FREE

Not only do the walnuts in this recipe add a nice bit of texture to a batch of otherwise moist and tender banana spice muffins, but they also contribute healthy fats and antioxidants that are extremely important for heart and brain health.

YIELD: 10-12 MUFFINS

1½ cups (121 g) rolled oats (quick or old-fashioned)

3 tbsp (21 g) ground flaxseed

1 tsp ground cinnamon

½ tsp ground nutmeg

2 tsp (8 g) baking powder

1 tsp baking soda

¼ tsp salt

2 large eggs

¼ cup (59 ml) unsweetened almond milk

¼ cup (64 g) almond butter

¼ cup (85 g) honey

2 tsp (10 ml) vanilla extract

2 medium-sized ripe bananas, mashed (about 1 cup [200 g])

½ cup (58 g) chopped walnuts

Preheat your oven to 350°F (177°C) and prepare a muffin pan by lining the cavities with parchment paper liners. Set aside.

Add the oats, ground flaxseed, cinnamon, nutmeg, baking powder, baking soda and salt to a high-speed blender, and process on high for about 10 seconds or until the oats have broken down into the consistency of a fine flour.

Add all of the remaining ingredients except for the bananas and walnuts, and process on high for about 30 seconds or until the batter becomes smooth and creamy. Periodically stop and scrape down the sides of your blender, if necessary. Finally, fold in the mashed bananas and walnuts by hand.

Spoon the batter into the prepared muffin cups, filling each one about ¾ of the way full. Sprinkle the tops with additional walnut pieces, if desired.

Bake for 18-20 minutes, until the tops of your muffins begin to turn golden brown and a toothpick inserted into the center comes out clean. Allow the muffins to cool in the pan for 10 minutes before transferring them to a wire rack to cool completely. As soon as they've cooled, transfer them to an airtight container and store them at room temperature for up to 5 days, or freeze for up to 3 months.

Morning Glory Muffins

GLUTEN-FREE, OIL-FREE, DAIRY-FREE, REFINED SUGAR-FREE

If these hearty little muffins were cars, they'd be rocking "fully loaded" labels.
With plenty of wholesome and delicious ingredients like oats, carrots, apples, raisins and nuts,
they're a delight not only for the taste buds, but the body as well.

YIELD: 10-12 MUFFINS

1½ cups (121 g) rolled oats (quick or old-fashioned)

3 tbsp (21 g) ground flaxseed

1 tsp ground cinnamon

½ tsp ground ginger

2 tsp (8 g) baking powder

1 tsp baking soda

½ tsp salt

3 large eggs

¾ cup (177 ml) unsweetened applesauce

6 tbsp (96 g) almond butter

¼ cup (85 g) honey

2 tsp (10 ml) vanilla extract

1 cup (115 g) shredded carrots

½ cup (76 g) raisins, soaked in warm water for 10 minutes and patted dry

½ cup (58 g) chopped walnuts

Preheat your oven to 350°F (177°C) and prepare a muffin pan by lining the cavities with parchment paper liners. Set aside.

Add the oats, ground flaxseed, cinnamon, ginger, baking powder, baking soda and salt to a high-speed blender, and process on high for about 10 seconds or until the oats have broken down into the consistency of a fine flour.

Add the eggs, applesauce, almond butter, honey and vanilla extract, and process on high for about 30 seconds or until the batter becomes smooth and creamy. Periodically stop and scrape down the sides of your blender, if necessary.

Transfer the batter to a medium-sized mixing bowl (this makes it easier to mix in the remaining ingredients), and fold in the carrots, raisins and walnuts by hand.

Spoon the batter into the prepared muffin cups, filling each one about ¾ of the way full.

Bake for 18-20 minutes, until the tops of your muffins begin to turn golden brown and a toothpick inserted into the center comes out clean. Allow the muffins to cool in the pan for 10 minutes before transferring them to a wire rack to cool completely. As soon as they've cooled, transfer them to an airtight container and store them at room temperature for up to 5 days, or freeze for up to 3 months.

Spiced Carrot Muffins

GLUTEN–FREE, OIL–FREE, DAIRY–FREE, REFINED SUGAR–FREE

The first time I used carrots in baking was when my mom requested a carrot cake for one of her birthdays. I didn't grow up loving veggies, and prior to that I would have said that they don't belong anywhere near my snacks or desserts. Boy was I wrong! Shredded carrots make an amazing addition to baked goods! Not only do they add a delicious, subtle sweetness to these healthy flourless muffins, but they make them nice and plump as well.

YIELD: 10–12 MUFFINS

1½ cups (121 g) rolled oats (quick or old-fashioned)

3 tbsp (21 g) ground flaxseed

1 tsp ground cinnamon

½ tsp ground ginger

¼ tsp ground nutmeg

2 tsp (8 g) baking powder

1 tsp baking soda

½ tsp salt

3 large eggs

½ cup (118 ml) pure orange juice

6 tbsp (96 g) almond butter

6 tbsp (89 ml) maple syrup

2 tsp (10 ml) vanilla extract

1 cup (115 g) shredded carrots

Preheat your oven to 350°F (177°C) and prepare a muffin pan by lining the cavities with parchment paper liners. Set aside.

Add the oats, ground flaxseed, cinnamon, ginger, nutmeg, baking powder, baking soda and salt to a high-speed blender, and process on high for about 10 seconds or until the oats have broken down into the consistency of a fine flour.

Add all of the remaining ingredients except for the carrots and process on high for about 30 seconds or until the batter becomes smooth and creamy. Periodically stop and scrape down the sides of your blender, if necessary. Finally, fold in the carrots by hand.

Spoon the batter into the prepared muffin cups, filling each one about ¾ of the way full.

Bake for 17–19 minutes, until the tops of your muffins begin to turn golden brown and a toothpick inserted into the center comes out clean. Allow the muffins to cool in the pan for 10 minutes before transferring them to a wire rack to cool completely. As soon as they've cooled, transfer them to an airtight container and store them at room temperature for up to 5 days, or freeze for up to 3 months.

Lemon Poppy Seed Muffins

GLUTEN-FREE, OIL-FREE, DAIRY-FREE, REFINED SUGAR-FREE

I remember being super skeptical the first time I tried a lemon muffin. I was (and still am) a fiend for chocolate, and the idea of a tart citrus fruit in what was supposed to be a sweet, doughy muffin just didn't sit well with me. But I couldn't have been more wrong! The lemon in these healthy flourless muffins adds a light and bright freshness, which pairs perfectly with the earthy nuttiness of the poppy seeds.

YIELD: 10–12 MUFFINS

1½ cups (121 g) rolled oats (quick or old-fashioned)

2 tbsp (14 g) ground flaxseed

2 tsp (8 g) baking powder

¾ tsp baking soda

¼ tsp salt

3 large eggs

¼ cup (59 ml) unsweetened almond milk

6 tbsp (96 g) almond butter

6 tbsp (128 g) honey

¼ cup (59 ml) lemon juice

2 tsp (10 ml) vanilla extract

2 tbsp (12 g) lemon zest

2 tbsp (17 g) poppy seeds

Preheat your oven to 350°F (177°C) and prepare a muffin pan by lining the cavities with parchment paper liners. Set aside.

Add the oats, ground flaxseed, baking powder, baking soda and salt to a high-speed blender, and process on high for about 10 seconds or until the oats have broken down into the consistency of a fine flour.

Add all of the remaining ingredients except for the lemon zest and poppy seeds, and process on high for about 30 seconds or until the batter becomes smooth and creamy. Periodically stop and scrape down the sides of your blender, if necessary. Add the lemon zest and poppy seeds to the batter and process on low for a few seconds or just until they become evenly distributed.

Spoon the batter into the prepared muffin cups, filling each one about ¾ of the way full.

Bake for 15–18 minutes, until the tops of your muffins begin to turn golden brown and a toothpick inserted into the center comes out clean. Allow the muffins to cool in the pan for 10 minutes before transferring them to a wire rack to cool completely. As soon as they've cooled, transfer them to an airtight container and store them at room temperature for up to 5 days, or freeze for up to 3 months.

Chocolate Chip Pumpkin Spice Muffins

GLUTEN-FREE, OIL-FREE, DAIRY-FREE OPTION*

Promise not to judge me when I admit that I didn't know pumpkin was edible until my mid-twenties? I grew up in a Polish family that didn't really do pumpkin pie for Thanksgiving, and it wasn't until I started reading food blogs that I was introduced to the nutritional powerhouse that is pumpkin. Since then, I haven't been able to get enough, and one of my absolute favorite ways to enjoy it is with chocolate and warming spices.

YIELD: 10–12 MUFFINS

1½ cups (121 g) rolled oats (quick or old-fashioned)

3 tbsp (21 g) ground flaxseed

1 tsp ground cinnamon

½ tsp ground nutmeg

½ tsp ground ginger

2 tsp (8 g) baking powder

¾ tsp baking soda

¼ tsp salt

2 large eggs

¼ cup (59 ml) unsweetened almond milk

¼ cup (64 g) almond butter

6 tbsp (128 g) honey

2 tsp (10 ml) vanilla extract

¾ cup (175 g) canned pumpkin puree

½ cup (90 g) semisweet chocolate chips (*for dairy-free, use vegan chocolate chips)

Preheat your oven to 350°F (177°C) and prepare a muffin pan by lining the cavities with parchment paper liners. Set aside.

Add the oats, ground flaxseed, cinnamon, nutmeg, ginger, baking powder, baking soda and salt to a high-speed blender, and process on high for about 10 seconds or until the oats have broken down into the consistency of a fine flour.

Add all of the remaining ingredients except for the chocolate chips, and process on high for about 30 seconds or until the batter becomes smooth and creamy. Periodically stop and scrape down the sides of your blender, if necessary. Finally, fold in the chocolate chips by hand.

Spoon the batter into the prepared muffin cups, filling each one about ¾ of the way full. Sprinkle the tops with additional chocolate chips, if desired.

Bake for 17–19 minutes, until the tops of your muffins begin to turn golden brown and a toothpick inserted into the center comes out clean. Allow the muffins to cool in the pan for 10 minutes before transferring them to a wire rack to cool completely. As soon as they've cooled, transfer them to an airtight container and store them at room temperature for up to 5 days, or freeze for up to 3 months.

Gingerbread Muffins

GLUTEN-FREE, OIL-FREE, DAIRY-FREE, REFINED SUGAR-FREE

These slightly more mature-tasting muffins are perfect for those who enjoy a little bit of extra spice in their lives. With plenty of warming spices like ginger, cinnamon, nutmeg and cloves, they make a great muffin to cozy up to in the evening along with a warm cup of tea or hot chocolate. And to intensify the spice flavor even further, you can buy spices in their whole form and grind them down yourself.

YIELD: 10-12 MUFFINS

1½ cups (121 g) rolled oats (quick or old-fashioned)

3 tbsp (21 g) ground flaxseed

2 tsp (5 g) ground ginger

1 tsp ground cinnamon

¼ tsp ground nutmeg

¼ tsp ground cloves

2 tsp (8 g) baking powder

1 tsp baking soda

¼ tsp salt

3 large eggs

½ cup (118 ml) unsweetened almond milk

6 tbsp (96 g) almond butter

¼ cup (88 g) molasses

¼ cup (85 g) honey

1 tsp vanilla extract

Preheat your oven to 350°F (177°C) and prepare a muffin pan by lining the cavities with parchment paper liners. Set aside.

Add the oats, ground flaxseed, ginger, cinnamon, nutmeg, cloves, baking powder, baking soda and salt to a high-speed blender, and process on high for about 10 seconds or until the oats have broken down into the consistency of a fine flour.

Add all of the remaining ingredients and process on high for about 30 seconds or until the batter becomes smooth and creamy. Periodically stop and scrape down the sides of your blender, if necessary.

Spoon the batter into the prepared muffin cups, filling each one about ¾ of the way full.

Bake for 17-19 minutes, until a toothpick inserted into the center comes out clean. Allow the muffins to cool in the pan for 10 minutes before transferring them to a wire rack to cool completely. As soon as they've cooled, transfer them to an airtight container and store them at room temperature for up to 5 days, or freeze for up to 3 months.

Orange Cranberry Muffins

GLUTEN-FREE, OIL-FREE, DAIRY-FREE, REFINED SUGAR-FREE

While they can definitely be enjoyed at any time of the year, these muffins always make me think of Christmas. The tartness of the cranberries is balanced out perfectly by the sweetness of the oranges, while warming spices add an irresistible richness and depth of flavor. To fancy them up a little more, you can make a glaze by combining powdered sugar with a little bit of water and drizzling it over the tops.

YIELD: 10–12 MUFFINS

2 cups (161 g) rolled oats (quick or old-fashioned)

3 tbsp (21 g) ground flaxseed

½ tsp ground cinnamon

½ tsp ground ginger

½ tsp ground nutmeg

2 tsp (8 g) baking powder

1 tsp baking soda

¼ tsp salt

3 large eggs

⅓ cup (78 ml) pure orange juice

6 tbsp (96 g) almond butter

½ cup (170 g) honey

1 tbsp (15 ml) vanilla extract

1 cup (99 g) cranberries, fresh or frozen

2 tsp (6 g) orange zest

Preheat your oven to 350°F (177°C) and prepare a muffin pan by lining the cavities with parchment paper liners. Set aside.

Add the oats, ground flaxseed, cinnamon, ginger, nutmeg, baking powder, baking soda and salt to a high-speed blender, and process on high for about 10 seconds or until the oats have broken down into the consistency of a fine flour.

Add all of the remaining ingredients except for the cranberries and orange zest, and process on high for about 30 seconds or until the batter becomes smooth and creamy. Periodically stop and scrape down the sides of your blender, if necessary. Finally, fold in the cranberries and orange zest by hand.

Spoon the batter into the prepared muffin cups, filling each one about ¾ of the way full.

Bake for 18–20 minutes, until the tops of your muffins begin to turn golden brown and a toothpick inserted into the center comes out clean. Allow the muffins to cool in the pan for 10 minutes before transferring them to a wire rack to cool completely. As soon as they've cooled, transfer them to an airtight container and store them at room temperature for up to 5 days, or freeze for up to 3 months.

NOTE

You can use dried cranberries if you don't have any fresh or frozen ones. Use ½ cup (80 g) and look for ones that have been sweetened with fruit juice if you want them to remain refined sugar-free.

Breakfast Muffins

While I may be a little biased seeing as it just so happens to be my favorite meal of the day, I'd gladly agree with the common belief that breakfast is the most important meal of the day. And at the very least, it's definitely the most delicious. Unfortunately, it's also the one that most readily gets skipped over when life gets busy, which is why it's never a bad idea to keep something on hand that's easy to grab on your way out the door—something nutritious that you can make ahead of time and store until needed. Something like the muffins you'll find in this chapter.

From the ever-popular Banana Oat Greek Yogurt Muffins (page 41) that so many of my readers have adopted as part of their morning routines, to healthy Cookie Dough Baked Oatmeal Cups (page 46) that'll make you feel like you're eating a mini deep-dish cookie for breakfast, each one of these recipes makes for a delicious and nutritious gluten-free breakfast option on those mornings where you find yourself rushing out the door after squeezing in those extra 20 minutes of sleep.

Banana Oat Greek Yogurt Muffins

GLUTEN-FREE, OIL-FREE

These muffins are, without a doubt, the most popular recipe on my blog, and I had to include them in this book because they are a healthy and delicious breakfast (or snack) that everyone needs in their life. The yogurt and bananas remove the need for any added oil or fat. The chocolate chips satisfy cravings and make you feel like you're still indulging in a nice little treat. If you want to make them even healthier or add a little bit of variety, you can replace the chocolate chips with berries or dried fruit.

YIELD: 12 MUFFINS

1 cup (227 g) plain Greek yogurt

2 medium-sized ripe bananas, mashed (about 1 cup [200 g])

2 large eggs

2 cups (161 g) rolled oats (quick or old-fashioned)

¼ cup (50 g) coconut palm sugar

2 tsp (10 ml) vanilla extract

1½ tsp (6 g) baking powder

½ tsp baking soda

½ cup (90 g) semisweet chocolate chips

Preheat your oven to 400°F (205°C) and prepare a muffin pan by lining the cavities with parchment paper liners. Set aside.

Add all of the ingredients except for the chocolate chips to a high-speed blender, and process on high until the oats have fully broken down and the batter is smooth and creamy, about 30-40 seconds. Periodically stop and scrape down the sides of your blender, if necessary. Finally, stir in the chocolate chips by hand.

Spoon the batter into the prepared muffin cups, filling each one about ¾ of the way full.

Sprinkle the tops with additional chocolate chips, if desired.

Bake for 15-18 minutes, until the tops of your muffins begin to turn golden brown and a toothpick inserted into the center comes out clean. Allow the muffins to cool in the pan for 10 minutes before transferring to a wire rack to cool completely. As soon as they've cooled, transfer them to an airtight container and store them at room temperature for up to 5 days, or freeze for up to 3 months.

NOTES

You could also use a flavored Greek yogurt, but this will slightly alter the taste of the finished product.

You could easily sub the coconut palm sugar with brown sugar.

Double Blueberry Banana Muffins

GLUTEN-FREE, OIL-FREE, DAIRY-FREE, REFINED SUGAR-FREE OPTION*

If you love blueberry muffins, then you're going to LOVE the double dose of berries in these soft and tender banana muffins. With whole berries incorporated into the batter and a swirl of blueberry jam baked on top, they not only look super fancy, but they're also loaded with antioxidants and blueberry flavor in each bite.

YIELD: 10-12 MUFFINS

1½ cups (121 g) rolled oats (quick or old-fashioned)

3 tbsp (21 g) ground flaxseed

1½ tsp (6 g) baking powder

½ tsp baking soda

¼ tsp salt

2 large eggs

¼ cup (59 ml) unsweetened almond milk

¼ cup (64 g) almond butter

¼ cup (85 g) honey

2 tsp (10 ml) vanilla extract

2 medium-sized ripe bananas, mashed (about 1 cup [200 g])

¾ cup (105 g) blueberries, fresh or frozen

1 tbsp (7 g) coconut flour

2 tbsp (30 ml) blueberry jam (*for refined sugar-free, use a jam sweetened with fruit juice)

Preheat your oven to 350°F (177°C) and prepare a muffin pan by lining the cavities with parchment paper liners. Set aside.

Add the oats, ground flaxseed, baking powder, baking soda and salt to a high-speed blender and process on high until the oats have broken down into the consistency of a fine flour, about 10 seconds.

Add all of the remaining ingredients except for the mashed bananas, blueberries, coconut flour and jam, and process on high for about 30 seconds or until the batter becomes smooth and creamy. Periodically stop and scrape down the sides of your blender, if necessary. Fold in the mashed bananas by hand.

Transfer the batter to a medium-sized mixing bowl (this makes it easier to prevent the berries from bleeding). Toss the blueberries in the 1 tablespoon (7 g) of coconut flour to prevent them from sinking to the bottom of the muffins, and gently fold them into the batter.

Spoon the batter into the prepared muffin cups, filling each one about ¾ of the way full. Top each muffin with ½ teaspoon of jam, and use a toothpick to swirl it around.

Bake for 17–19 minutes, until the tops of your muffins begin to turn golden brown and a toothpick inserted into the center comes out clean. Allow the muffins to cool in the pan for 10 minutes before transferring them to a wire rack to cool completely. As soon as they've cooled, transfer them to an airtight container and store them at room temperature for up to 5 days, or freeze for up to 3 months.

Green Smoothie Muffins

GLUTEN-FREE, OIL-FREE, DAIRY-FREE, REFINED SUGAR-FREE OPTION*

Don't let the unique color of these muffins scare you! The green hue comes from baby spinach that's smoothly blended into the batter, which has such a mild flavor that you can hardly tell it's there. Instead, you get a tender banana-flavored muffin with a hint of "freshness" and the added bonus of some vitamins and minerals thrown in!

YIELD: 10-12 MUFFINS

1½ cups (121 g) rolled oats (quick or old-fashioned)

3 tbsp (21 g) ground flaxseed

2 tsp (8 g) baking powder

½ tsp baking soda

¼ tsp salt

2 large eggs

2 medium-sized ripe bananas (about 1 cup [200 g])

1½ cups (42 g) fresh baby spinach

6 tbsp (96 g) almond butter

5 tbsp (107 g) honey

1 tsp vanilla extract

½ cup (90 g) chocolate chips, optional (*for refined sugar-free, leave them out)

Preheat your oven to 350°F (177°C) and prepare a muffin pan by lining the cavities with parchment paper liners. Set aside.

Add the oats, ground flaxseed, baking powder, baking soda and salt to a high-speed blender, and process on high for about 10 seconds or until the oats have broken down into the consistency of a fine flour.

Add all of the remaining ingredients except for the chocolate chips, if using, and process on high for about 30-40 seconds or until the batter becomes smooth and creamy. Periodically stop and scrape down the sides of your blender, as necessary. Finally, if using, fold in the chocolate chips by hand.

Spoon the batter into the prepared muffin cups, filling each one about ¾ of the way full. Sprinkle the tops with additional chocolate chips, if using.

Bake for 18-20 minutes, until a toothpick inserted into the center comes out clean. Allow the muffins to cool in the pan for 10 minutes before transferring them to a wire rack to cool completely. As soon as they've cooled, transfer them to an airtight container and store them at room temperature for up to 5 days, or freeze for up to 3 months.

Cookie Dough Baked Oatmeal Cups

GLUTEN-FREE, OIL-FREE, DAIRY-FREE OPTION*

Who says you can't eat cookies for breakfast? These healthy baked oatmeal cups have that delicious chocolate chip cookie taste but boast the healthy ingredients that we normally find at the breakfast table, like oats, almonds, apples and maple syrup. To make them even healthier, you can replace the chocolate chips with dried fruit or nuts.

YIELD: 10 MUFFIN CUPS

2 cups (161 g) old-fashioned rolled oats

¼ cup (28 g) almond flour

1½ tsp (6 g) baking powder

1 large egg

½ cup (118 ml) unsweetened almond milk

¼ cup (64 g) almond butter

¼ cup (59 ml) maple syrup

¼ cup (59 ml) unsweetened applesauce

1 tsp vanilla extract

⅓ cup (59 g) semisweet chocolate chips (*for dairy-free, use vegan chocolate chips)

Preheat your oven to 350°F (177°C) and prepare a muffin pan by lining the cavities with parchment paper liners. Set aside.

In a large mixing bowl, combine the oats, almond flour and baking powder. Set aside.

In a medium-sized mixing bowl, whisk together all the remaining ingredients except for the chocolate chips. Add the wet ingredients to the dry ingredients and mix until well combined before folding in the chocolate chips. The batter will be very loose and wet.

Spoon the batter into the prepared muffin cups, filling each one to the very top.

Bake for 22–25 minutes, until the tops of your muffin cups begin to turn golden brown and a toothpick inserted into the center comes out clean. Allow the muffin cups to cool in the pan for 10 minutes before transferring them to a wire rack to cool completely. As soon as they've cooled, transfer them to an airtight container, and store them at room temperature for up to 5 days, or freeze for up to 3 months.

NOTES

For best results, use a finely ground almond flour made from blanched almonds.

You could also use honey or agave nectar in place of the maple syrup.

Strawberry Banana Muffins

GLUTEN-FREE, OIL-FREE, DAIRY-FREE, REFINED SUGAR-FREE

These healthy muffins taste like summer—light, fresh, fruity and sweet. They're the perfect way to enjoy the abundance of fresh berries that come around every summer, and you can easily replace the strawberries with raspberries, blueberries, blackberries or any other berry that you love.

YIELD: 10–12 MUFFINS

1½ cups (121 g) rolled oats (quick or old-fashioned)

3 tbsp (21 g) ground flaxseed

1½ tsp (6 g) baking powder

½ tsp baking soda

¼ tsp salt

2 large eggs

¼ cup (59 ml) unsweetened almond milk

¼ cup (64 g) almond butter

¼ cup (85 g) honey

2 tsp (10 ml) vanilla extract

2 medium-sized ripe bananas, mashed (about 1 cup [200 g])

1 cup (151 g) diced strawberries, fresh or frozen

Preheat your oven to 350°F (177°C) and prepare a muffin pan by lining the cavities with parchment paper liners. Set aside.

Add the oats, ground flaxseed, baking powder, baking soda and salt to a high-speed blender, and process on high for about 10 seconds or until the oats have broken down into the consistency of a fine flour.

Add all of the remaining ingredients except for the mashed bananas and diced strawberries, and process on high for about 30 seconds until the batter becomes smooth and creamy. Periodically stop and scrape down the sides of your blender, if necessary. Fold in the mashed bananas by hand.

Transfer the batter to a medium-sized mixing bowl (this makes it easier to prevent the berries from bleeding), and gently fold the strawberries into the batter.

Spoon the batter into the prepared muffin cups, filling each one about ¾ of the way full.

Bake for 19–21 minutes, until the tops of your muffins begin to turn golden brown and a toothpick inserted into the center comes out clean. Allow the muffins to cool in the pan for 10 minutes before transferring them to a wire rack to cool completely. As soon as they've cooled, transfer them to an airtight container and store them at room temperature for up to 5 days, or freeze for up to 3 months.

Zucchini Banana Bread Muffins

GLUTEN-FREE, OIL-FREE, DAIRY-FREE, REFINED SUGAR-FREE

These subtly sweet muffins are impossibly tender thanks to a batter that's loaded with both mashed banana and shredded zucchini. If you're baking for picky eaters, you might want to peel your zucchini prior to shredding so that it'll be harder to detect. Otherwise, I like to leave the peel on for some extra vitamins. That and I just think the little green specs look so pretty!

YIELD: 10-12 MUFFINS

1½ cups (121 g) rolled oats (quick or old-fashioned)

2 tbsp (14 g) ground flaxseed

½ tsp ground cinnamon

2 tsp (8 g) baking powder

½ tsp baking soda

¼ tsp salt

2 large eggs

6 tbsp (96 g) almond butter

6 tbsp (128 g) honey

2 tsp (10 ml) vanilla extract

2 medium-sized ripe bananas, mashed (about 1 cup [200 g])

1 cup (115 g) shredded zucchini, squeezed of excess liquid

Preheat your oven to 350°F (177°C) and prepare a muffin pan by lining the cavities with parchment paper liners. Set aside.

Add the oats, ground flaxseed, cinnamon, baking powder, baking soda and salt to a high-speed blender, and process on high for about 10 seconds or until the oats have broken down into the consistency of a fine flour.

Add all of the remaining ingredients except for the bananas and zucchini, and process on high for about 30 seconds or until the batter becomes smooth and creamy. Periodically stop and scrape down the sides of your blender, if necessary.

Transfer the batter to a medium-sized mixing bowl (this makes it easier to mix in the remaining ingredients), and fold in the bananas and zucchini by hand.

Spoon the batter into the prepared muffin cups, filling each one about ¾ of the way full.

Bake for 18-20 minutes, until the tops of your muffins begin to turn golden brown and a toothpick inserted into the center comes out clean. Allow the muffins to cool in the pan for 10 minutes before transferring them to a wire rack to cool completely. As soon as they've cooled, transfer them to an airtight container and store them at room temperature for up to 5 days, or freeze for up to 3 months.

NOTE

I like to place a handful of shredded zucchini between two paper towels and squeeze it over the sink. This drains it of just the right amount of liquid to allow the muffins to cook properly.

Almond Butter and Jelly Muffins

GLUTEN-FREE, OIL-FREE, DAIRY-FREE, REFINED SUGAR-FREE OPTION*

I opted to use almond butter in this recipe because I have a pesky allergy to peanuts, but feel free to replace it with peanut butter to enjoy the classic taste of PB&J! If you're dealing with a nut allergy? No problem! You can use soy nut butter and different non-dairy milk like rice or soy to make these nut-free.

YIELD: 10-12 MUFFINS

1½ cups (121 g) rolled oats (quick or old-fashioned)

3 tbsp (21 g) ground flaxseed

1½ tsp (6 g) baking powder

½ tsp baking soda

¼ tsp salt

2 large eggs

¼ cup (59 ml) unsweetened almond milk

½ cup (128 g) almond butter, plus more for topping

6 tbsp (128 g) honey

2 tsp (10 ml) vanilla extract

2-3 tbsp (30-45 ml) jelly or jam of choice (*for refined sugar-free, use a jam that's sweetened with fruit juice)

Preheat your oven to 350°F (177°C) and prepare a muffin pan by lining the cavities with parchment paper liners. Set aside.

Add the oats, ground flaxseed, baking powder, baking soda and salt to a high-speed blender and process on high for about 10 seconds or until the oats have broken down into the consistency of a fine flour.

Add all of the remaining ingredients except for the jam, and process on high for about 30 seconds or until the batter becomes smooth and creamy. Periodically stop and scrape down the sides of your blender, as necessary.

Spoon the batter into the prepared muffin cups, filling each one about ¾ of the way full. Top each muffin with ½ teaspoon of jam and ¼ teaspoon of almond butter, and use a toothpick to swirl them around.

Bake for 18-20 minutes, until the tops of your muffins begin to turn golden brown and a toothpick inserted into the center comes out clean. Allow the muffins to cool in the pan for 10 minutes before transferring them to a wire rack to cool completely. As soon as they've cooled, transfer them to an airtight container and store them at room temperature for up to 5 days, or freeze for up to 3 months.

Trail Mix Muffins

GLUTEN–FREE, OIL–FREE, DAIRY–FREE OPTION*

I know I'm not the only one who has a hard time controlling herself around trail mix, especially when it comes to picking out my favorite ingredients. One of the best things about these soft and fluffy muffins is that you can customize the add-ins based on your favorite trail mix ingredients, or switch them up with each new batch always having something different.

YIELD: 10–12 MUFFINS

1 cup (80 g) rolled oats (quick or old-fashioned)

3 tbsp (21 g) ground flaxseed

2 tsp (8 g) baking powder

½ tsp baking soda

¼ tsp salt

3 large eggs

¼ cup (59 ml) unsweetened almond milk

6 tbsp (96 g) almond butter

¼ cup (85 g) honey

1 tsp vanilla extract

½ cup (70 g) pumpkin or sunflower seeds

½ cup (80 g) dried fruit of choice

½ cup (40 g) old-fashioned rolled oats

¼ cup (45 g) mini chocolate chips (*for dairy-free, use vegan chocolate chips)

Preheat your oven to 350°F (177°C) and prepare a muffin pan by lining the cavities with parchment paper liners. Set aside.

Add the oats, ground flaxseed, baking powder, baking soda and salt to a high-speed blender, and process on high for about 10 seconds or until the oats have broken down into the consistency of a fine flour.

Add the eggs, almond milk, almond butter, honey and vanilla, and process on high for about 30 seconds or until the batter becomes smooth and creamy. Periodically stop and scrape down the sides of your blender, if necessary.

Transfer the batter to a medium-sized mixing bowl and fold in all the remaining ingredients.

Spoon the batter into the prepared muffin cups, filling each one about ¾ of the way full. Sprinkle the tops with additional seeds, dried fruit, oats and chocolate chips, if desired.

Bake for 15–18 minutes, until the tops of your muffins begin to turn golden brown and a toothpick inserted into the center comes out clean. Allow the muffins to cool in the pan for 10 minutes before transferring them to a wire rack to cool completely. As soon as they've cooled, transfer them to an airtight container and store them at room temperature for up to 5 days, or freeze for up to 3 months.

Honey Almond Oatmeal Muffins

GLUTEN-FREE, OIL-FREE, DAIRY-FREE, REFINED SUGAR-FREE

Did you know that different honeys have different flavors depending on what kind of flowers the honeybees were visiting? My absolute favorite is buckwheat honey, which has a slightly stronger and more robust flavor that really shines through in baked goods. It also pairs perfectly with the subtly sweet taste of almonds in these flourless muffins.

YIELD: 10-12 MUFFINS

1¾ cups (141 g) rolled oats (quick or old-fashioned), divided

2 tbsp (14 g) ground flaxseed

1½ tsp (6 g) baking powder

½ tsp baking soda

¼ tsp salt

2 large eggs

½ cup (118 ml) unsweetened almond milk

½ cup (128 g) almond butter

½ cup (170 g) honey

½ tsp almond extract

¼ cup (28 g) almond flour

¼ cup (25 g) sliced blanched almonds, for topping

Preheat your oven to 350°F (177°C) and prepare a muffin pan by lining the cavities with parchment paper liners. Set aside.

Add ¾ cup (60 g) oats, ground flaxseed, baking powder, baking soda and salt to a high-speed blender, and process on high for about 10 seconds until the oats have broken down into the consistency of a fine flour.

Add all of the remaining ingredients except for the reserved oats, almond flour and sliced almonds, and process on high for about 30 seconds or until the batter becomes smooth and creamy. Periodically stop and scrape down the sides of your blender, if necessary. The batter will be somewhat thin and runny. This is normal—the remaining oats will soak up a lot of the liquid and thicken the batter.

Transfer the batter to a medium-sized mixing bowl and fold in the remaining oats and almond flour by hand, mixing well to ensure that everything becomes fully incorporated. Let the batter sit for about 10 minutes to give the oats a chance to soften and soak up some of the liquid.

Spoon the batter into the prepared muffin cups, filling each one about ¾ of the way full. Sprinkle the tops with sliced almonds.

Bake for 15-18 minutes, until the tops of your muffins begin to turn golden brown and a toothpick inserted into the center comes out clean. Allow the muffins to cool in the pan for 10 minutes before transferring them to a wire rack to cool completely. As soon as they've cooled, transfer them to an airtight container and store them at room temperature for up to 5 days, or freeze for up to 3 months.

Tropical Baked Oatmeal Cups

GLUTEN–FREE, OIL–FREE, DAIRY–FREE, REFINED SUGAR–FREE

These individually-sized baked oatmeal cups make an irresistible breakfast-to-go thanks to their ultra-moist texture and subtly sweet tropical flavor. You can also switch out the mango for any other fruit you have on hand to keep things fresh and interesting!

YIELD: 12 MUFFIN CUPS

2 cups (161 g) old-fashioned rolled oats

½ cup (38 g) unsweetened coconut, shredded or flaked

1½ tsp (6 g) baking powder

1 large egg

½ cup (118 ml) unsweetened almond milk

¼ cup (59 ml) light canned coconut milk

¼ cup (85 g) honey

2 medium-sized ripe bananas, mashed (about 1 cup [200 g])

½ tsp almond extract

1 cup (100 g) diced mango, fresh or frozen

Preheat your oven to 350°F (177°C) and prepare a muffin pan by lining the cavities with parchment paper liners. Set aside.

In a large mixing bowl, combine the oats, shredded coconut and baking powder. Set aside.

In a medium-sized mixing bowl, whisk together the all the remaining ingredients except for the diced mango. Add the wet ingredients to the dry ingredients and mix until well combined before folding in the diced mango. The batter will be very loose and wet.

Spoon the batter into the prepared muffin cups, filling each one to the very top.

Bake for 25–30 minutes, until the tops of your muffin cups begin to turn golden brown and a toothpick inserted into the center comes out clean. Allow the muffin cups to cool in the pan for 10 minutes before transferring them to a wire rack to cool completely. As soon as they've cooled, transfer them to an airtight container and store them at room temperature for up to 5 days, or freeze for up to 3 months.

NOTE

If you don't have any coconut milk, you can use ¾ cup (180 ml) of unsweetened almond milk.

Honey Oat Ricotta Muffins

GLUTEN-FREE, OIL-FREE, REFINED SUGAR-FREE

Did you know that ricotta isn't technically a cheese since it's made from the whey that's left over from making other cheeses? This gives it a slightly sweeter taste and makes it absolutely perfect for baking. Not only does the ricotta help make these muffins super tender, but it also adds a nice little boost of calcium and protein. Drizzle these with additional honey just prior to eating for an extra special treat.

YIELD: 10–12 MUFFINS

2 cups (160 g) rolled oats (quick or old-fashioned), divided

2 tbsp (14 g) ground flaxseed

2 tsp (8 g) baking powder

1 tsp baking soda

1 tsp ground cinnamon

2 large eggs

¼ cup (64 g) almond butter

½ cup (170 g) honey

1 tsp vanilla extract

¾ cup (165 g) ricotta cheese (regular or light)

Preheat your oven to 350°F (177°C) and prepare a muffin pan by lining the cavities with parchment paper liners. Set aside.

Add 1½ cups (121 g) oats, ground flaxseed, baking powder, baking soda and cinnamon to a high-speed blender, and process on high for about 10 seconds or until the oats have broken down into the consistency of a fine flour.

Add all of the remaining ingredients except for the ricotta and remaining ½ cup (40 g) rolled oats and process on high for about 30 seconds or until the batter becomes smooth and creamy. Periodically stop and scrape down the sides of your blender, as necessary.

Transfer the batter to a medium-sized mixing bowl and fold in the ricotta cheese and remaining rolled oats by hand, mixing well to ensure that everything becomes fully incorporated.

Spoon the batter into the prepared muffin cups, filling each one about ¾ of the way full.

Bake for 15-17 minutes, until the tops of your muffins begin to turn golden brown and a toothpick inserted into the center comes out clean. Allow the muffins to cool in the pan for 10 minutes before transferring them to a wire rack to cool completely. As soon as they've cooled, transfer them to an airtight container and store them at room temperature for up to 5 days, or freeze for up to 3 months.

Coffeehouse Favorites

Is there anything better than enjoying a freshly baked muffin with your coffee or tea? Maybe enjoying one with an espresso at a street-side café in Paris . . . but, since we can't all be jetting off to France whenever we please, this is basically the next best thing. No, really!

All the muffins in this chapter have a little extra something that makes them perfect for those special occasions when only a little extra something will do. Going to a lovely Sunday brunch with your family? Why not bring a batch of Strawberry Cheesecake Muffins (page 69) for dessert? Having your girlfriends over for a relaxing night in? The Banana Pecan Crumble Muffins (page 81) would be the first to disappear from the snack table. Or maybe you just want to treat yourself after a rough week. Well, the Double Banana Chocolate Chip Streusel Muffins (page 66) are pretty darn good for that. No matter what your occasion, these muffins will undoubtedly make it more special. And the best part is that, despite their fanciness, they're all still incredibly easy to prepare and fit perfectly into any healthy diet.

Coffee Cake Greek Yogurt Muffins

GLUTEN-FREE

These muffins are what instantly come to mind when I think "quintessential coffee cake flavor."
The muffins themselves are pretty simple—light, sweet and oil-free thanks to the powers of Greek yogurt.
But the simple base is what lets the delicious cinnamon sugar topping shine. These are
definitely coffee's favorite muffins, and your body will love them, too!

YIELD: 10-12 MUFFINS

FOR THE MUFFINS

½ cup (114 g) plain Greek yogurt (fat-free or 2% is fine)

¼ cup (64 g) almond butter

2 large eggs

1½ cups (121 g) rolled oats (quick or old-fashioned)

¼ cup (85 g) honey

2 tbsp (30 ml) unsweetened applesauce

1 tsp ground cinnamon

2 tsp (8 g) baking powder

1 tsp baking soda

¼ tsp salt

2 tsp (10 ml) vanilla extract

FOR THE TOPPING

½ cup (40 g) old-fashioned rolled oats

¼ cup (28 g) almond flour

6 tbsp (75 g) coconut palm sugar

3 tbsp (44 ml) coconut oil, melted

½ tsp ground cinnamon

Preheat your oven to 350°F (177°C) and prepare a muffin pan by lining the cavities with parchment paper liners. Set aside.

Add all the muffin ingredients to a high-speed blender in the order listed and process on high until the oats have fully broken down and the batter becomes smooth and creamy, about 30-40 seconds. Periodically stop and scrape down the sides of your blender, as necessary.

Divide the batter evenly among the prepared muffin cups, filling each one about ⅔ of the way full. Set aside.

Combine all of the topping ingredients in a small bowl and liberally sprinkle it on top of each muffin.

Bake for 17-19 minutes, until the tops of your muffins begin to turn golden brown and a toothpick inserted into the center comes out clean. Allow the muffins to cool in the pan for 10 minutes before transferring them to a wire rack to cool completely. As soon as they've cooled, transfer them to an airtight container and store them at room temperature for up to 5 days, or freeze for up to 3 months.

NOTE

You could easily sub the coconut palm sugar with brown or granulated sugar.

Double Banana Chocolate Chip Streusel Muffins

GLUTEN-FREE, DAIRY-FREE OPTION*

With two bananas mashed in the batter and gooey banana chunks throughout, these muffins are perfect for the serious banana lover who can't get enough of the sweet and flavorful fruit. And the chocolate chip streusel is perfect for the chocolate lover who knows that the banana-chocolate combo is one of the best there is.

YIELD: 12 MUFFINS

FOR THE MUFFINS

1½ cups (121 g) rolled oats (quick or old-fashioned)

3 tbsp (21 g) ground flaxseed

½ tsp ground cinnamon

2 tsp (8 g) baking powder

½ tsp baking soda

¼ tsp salt

2 large eggs

2 medium-sized ripe bananas, mashed (about 1 cup [200 g])

¼ cup (59 ml) unsweetened almond milk

¼ cup (64 g) almond butter

¼ cup (85 g) honey

1 tsp vanilla extract

1 medium-sized firm and ripe banana, diced (about ½ cup [100 g])

FOR THE CHOCOLATE STREUSEL TOPPING

¼ cup (50 g) coconut palm sugar

2 tbsp (12 g) almond flour

2 tbsp (30 ml) coconut oil, melted

2 tbsp (10 g) old-fashioned rolled oats

½ cup (90 g) mini chocolate chips (*for dairy-free, use vegan chocolate chips)

Preheat your oven to 350°F (177°C) and prepare a muffin pan by lining the cavities with parchment paper liners. Set aside.

Add the oats, ground flaxseed, cinnamon, baking powder, baking soda and salt to a high-speed blender, and process on high for about 10 seconds or until the oats have broken down into the consistency of a fine flour.

Add all of the remaining muffin ingredients except for the diced banana and the chocolate streusel topping, and process on high for about 30 seconds or until the batter becomes smooth and creamy. Periodically stop and scrape down the sides of your blender, as necessary. Finally, fold in the diced banana by hand.

Spoon the batter into the prepared muffin cups, filling each one about ¾ of the way full. Prepare the topping by combining the sugar, flour and oil in a small bowl, then stirring in the oats and chocolate chips. Divide the topping evenly among all the muffins.

Bake for 20–22 minutes, until the tops of your muffins begin to turn golden brown and a toothpick inserted into the center comes out clean. Allow the muffins to cool in the pan for 10 minutes before transferring them to a wire rack to cool completely. As soon as they've cooled, transfer them to an airtight container and store them at room temperature for up to 5 days, or freeze for up to 3 months.

Strawberry Cheesecake Muffins

GLUTEN-FREE, OIL-FREE

If you're a fan of cheesecake, you're going to love these tender strawberry muffins with their sweet cheesecake swirl. If you're not a fan of cheesecake? You're still going to love these muffins since they remain light and fluffy rather than overly rich and dense. And the best part is that they look all fancy while being super easy to make. Or maybe the best part is that they allow you to satisfy your cheesecake cravings while sticking to your healthy diet.

YIELD: 10–12 MUFFINS

FOR THE MUFFINS

2 cups (161 g) rolled oats (quick or old-fashioned)

2 tbsp (14 g) ground flaxseed

2 tsp (8 g) baking powder

½ tsp baking soda

¼ tsp salt

2 large eggs

⅓ cup (78 ml) unsweetened almond milk

6 tbsp (96 g) almond butter

6 tbsp (128 g) honey

1 tbsp (15 ml) vanilla extract

1 cup (151 g) diced strawberries, fresh or frozen

FOR THE CREAM CHEESE TOPPING

6 oz (170 g) cream cheese, softened

1 egg yolk

¼ cup (48 g) cane or granulated sugar

Preheat your oven to 350°F (177°C) and prepare a muffin pan by lining the cavities with parchment paper liners. Set aside.

Add the oats, ground flaxseed, baking powder, baking soda and salt to a high-speed blender, and process on high for about 10 seconds or until the oats have broken down into the consistency of a fine flour.

Add all of the remaining muffin ingredients except for the strawberries, and process on high for about 30 seconds or until the batter becomes smooth and creamy. Periodically stop and scrape down the sides of your blender, if necessary.

Transfer the batter to a medium-sized mixing bowl (this makes it easier to prevent the berries from bleeding), and gently fold the strawberries into the batter.

Spoon the batter into the prepared muffin cups, filling each one about ¾ of the way full. In a medium-sized bowl, beat the cream cheese until it becomes smooth. Add the egg yolk and sugar, and continue beating until all the ingredients are combined. Top each muffin with 1 tablespoon (15 ml) of the cream cheese mixture, and use a toothpick to gently swirl it into the batter.

Bake for 22–24 minutes, until the tops of your muffins begin to turn golden brown and a toothpick inserted into the center comes out clean. Allow the muffins to cool in the pan for 10 minutes before transferring them to a wire rack to cool completely. As soon as they've cooled, transfer them to an airtight container and store them at room temperature for up to 5 days, or freeze for up to 3 months.

Cinnamon Sugar Crunch Muffins

GLUTEN-FREE, DAIRY-FREE

In addition to a sweet and crunchy cinnamon streusel topping infused with raisins and walnuts, these flourless muffins also have swirls of cinnamon sugar throughout. I like to use turbinado cane sugar since it's minimally refined and has larger crystals that add a nice crunch, but you can just as easily use brown sugar if that's what you have on hand.

YIELD: 10-12 MUFFINS

FOR THE MUFFINS

1½ cups (121 g) rolled oats (quick or old-fashioned)

3 tbsp (21 g) ground flaxseed

2 tsp (8 g) baking powder

1 tsp baking soda

¼ tsp salt

3 large eggs

¼ cup (59 ml) unsweetened almond milk

6 tbsp (96 g) almond butter

¼ cup (85 g) honey

FOR THE TOPPING/FILLING

¼ cup (50 g) turbinado cane sugar

1 tbsp (8 g) ground cinnamon

2 tbsp (30 ml) coconut oil, melted

½ cup (58 g) chopped walnuts

¼ cup (38 g) raisins

Preheat your oven to 350°F (177°C) and prepare a muffin pan by lining the cavities with parchment paper liners. Set aside.

Add the oats, ground flaxseed, baking powder, baking soda and salt to a high-speed blender, and process on high for about 10 seconds or until the oats have broken down into the consistency of a fine flour.

Add all of the remaining muffin ingredients, and process on high for about 30 seconds or until the batter becomes smooth and creamy. Periodically stop and scrape down the sides of your blender, if necessary.

Prepare the topping/filling by combining all of the ingredients in a small bowl. Transfer the muffin batter to a medium-sized mixing bowl (this makes it easier to mix in the filling), and gently fold half of the filling/topping mixture into the batter, not incorporating it fully, but simply swirling it around.

Spoon the batter into the prepared muffin cups, filling each one about ¾ of the way full. Divide the remaining filling/topping mixture evenly among the tops of all the muffins.

Bake for 20-22 minutes, until the tops of your muffins begin to turn golden brown and a toothpick inserted into the center comes out clean. Allow the muffins to cool in the pan for 10 minutes before transferring them to a wire rack to cool completely. As soon as they've cooled, transfer them to an airtight container and store them at room temperature for up to 5 days, or freeze for up to 3 months.

Toasted Coconut Honey Muffins

GLUTEN-FREE, OIL-FREE, DAIRY-FREE, REFINED SUGAR-FREE

While I usually like to keep things as simple as possible, and toasting coconut just seems like an unnecessary extra step, believe me when I say the 5 minutes it takes to toast coconut makes all the difference. Even if you're not a die-hard coconut fan, it's hard not to love the subtly sweet aromatic flavor that comes out as it turns golden brown. Pair that with a more robust honey variety like buckwheat, and you have a muffin that's an absolute joy for the senses.

YIELD: 10 MUFFINS

¾ cup (57 g) unsweetened coconut, shredded or flaked, divided

1¾ cup (141 g) rolled oats (quick or old-fashioned)

¼ cup (28 g) coconut flour

2 tsp (8 g) baking powder

1 tsp baking soda

¼ tsp salt

3 large eggs

½ cup (118 ml) canned light coconut milk

6 tbsp (128 g) honey

Add ½ cup (38 g) of the shredded coconut to a large dry pan set over medium heat. Cook it for around 5 minutes or until it begins to turn golden brown and fragrant, stirring constantly to prevent it from burning. Remove the pan from the heat and set it aside to allow the coconut to cool.

Preheat your oven to 325°F (163°C) and prepare a muffin pan by lining the cavities with parchment paper liners. Set aside.

Add the oats, coconut flour, baking powder, baking soda and salt to a high-speed blender, and process on high for about 10 seconds or until the oats have broken down into the consistency of a fine flour.

Add all of the remaining ingredients except for the reserved, untoasted coconut and the toasted coconut, and process on high for about 30 seconds or until the batter becomes smooth and creamy. Periodically stop and scrape down the sides of your blender, if necessary. Finally, fold in the toasted coconut by hand.

Spoon the batter into the prepared muffin cups, filling each one about ¾ of the way full. Liberally sprinkle the tops with the reserved, untoasted coconut.

Bake for 15-17 minutes, until the tops of your muffins begin to turn golden brown and a toothpick inserted into the center comes out clean. Allow the muffins to cool in the pan for 10 minutes before transferring them to a wire rack to cool completely. As soon as they've cooled, transfer them to an airtight container and store them at room temperature for up to 5 days, or freeze for up to 3 months.

Chunky Monkey Muffins

GLUTEN-FREE, OIL-FREE, DAIRY-FREE OPTION*

Unfortunately (or fortunately, maybe?), the "chunky monkey" in the title isn't referring to a slightly chubby primate. Instead, it brings to light the fact that these muffins feature the unarguably delicious flavor combination of bananas, chocolate and walnuts that Ben and Jerry's® made famous. I used a dark chocolate roughly cut up into chunks here, but feel free to use semisweet chocolate chips if you're not the biggest fan of the slightly bitter taste of dark chocolate.

YIELD: 10–12 MUFFINS

1½ cups (121 g) rolled oats (quick or old-fashioned)

3 tbsp (21 g) ground flaxseed

2 tsp (8 g) baking powder

1 tsp baking soda

½ tsp salt

2 large eggs

½ cup (118 ml) unsweetened almond milk

6 tbsp (96 g) almond butter

¼ cup (85 g) honey

1 tbsp (15 ml) vanilla extract

2 medium-sized ripe bananas, mashed (about 1 cup [200 g])

½ cup (58 g) chopped walnuts

½ cup (90 g) dark chocolate, roughly cut into chunks (*for dairy-free, use vegan dark chocolate)

Preheat your oven to 350°F (177°C) and prepare a muffin pan by lining the cavities with parchment paper liners. Set aside.

Add the oats, ground flaxseed, baking powder, baking soda and salt to a high-speed blender, and process on high for about 10 seconds or until the oats have broken down into the consistency of a fine flour.

Add the eggs, almond milk, almond butter, honey and vanilla, and process on high for about 30 seconds or until the batter becomes smooth and creamy. Periodically stop and scrape down the sides of your blender, if necessary. Finally, fold in the mashed bananas, walnuts and chocolate chips by hand.

Spoon the batter into the prepared muffin cups, filling each one about ¾ of the way full. Sprinkle the tops with additional chocolate chips, if desired.

Bake for 18–20 minutes, until the tops of your muffins begin to turn golden brown and a toothpick inserted into the center comes out clean. Allow the muffins to cool in the pan for 10 minutes before transferring them to a wire rack to cool completely. As soon as they've cooled, transfer them to an airtight container and store them at room temperature for up to 5 days, or freeze for up to 3 months.

Pumpkin Cream Cheese Muffins

GLUTEN-FREE, OIL-FREE

While I'm normally all about that pumpkin and chocolate combo, this cream cheese pairing is making a serious case for top spot! There's just something about its sweetly tart creaminess that's completely irresistible when paired with a spiced pumpkin muffin.

YIELD: 10–12 MUFFINS

FOR THE MUFFINS

1½ cups (121 g) rolled oats (quick or old-fashioned)

2 tbsp (14 g) ground flaxseed

1 tsp ground cinnamon

½ tsp ground nutmeg

½ tsp ground ginger

1½ tsp (6 g) baking powder

½ tsp baking soda

¼ tsp salt

2 large eggs

¼ cup (64 g) almond butter

6 tbsp (128 g) honey

2 tsp (10 ml) vanilla extract

¾ cup (175 g) canned pumpkin

FOR THE CREAM CHEESE TOPPING

6 oz (170 g) cream cheese, softened

1 egg yolk

¼ cup (48 g) cane or granulated sugar

Preheat your oven to 350°F (177°C) and prepare a muffin pan by lining the cavities with parchment paper liners. Set aside.

Add the oats, ground flaxseed, cinnamon, nutmeg, ginger, baking powder, baking soda and salt to a high-speed blender, and process on high for about 10 seconds or until the oats have broken down into the consistency of a fine flour.

Add all of the remaining muffin ingredients, and process on high for about 30 seconds or until the batter becomes smooth and creamy. Periodically stop and scrape down the sides of your blender, if necessary.

Spoon the batter into the prepared muffin cups, filling each one about ¾ of the way full. In a medium-sized bowl, beat the cream cheese until it becomes smooth. Add the egg yolk and sugar, and continue beating until all of the ingredients become well combined. Top each muffin with 1 tablespoon (15 g) of the cream cheese mixture, and use a toothpick to gently swirl it into the batter.

Bake for 22–24 minutes, until the tops of your muffins begin to turn golden brown and a toothpick inserted into the center comes out clean. Allow the muffins to cool in the pan for 10 minutes before transferring them to a wire rack to cool completely. As soon as they've cooled, transfer them to an airtight container and store them at room temperature for up to 5 days, or freeze for up to 3 months.

Almond Joy Muffins

GLUTEN-FREE, OIL-FREE, DAIRY-FREE OPTION*

Can we please take a moment to talk about the awesomeness that is almond extract? Because while vanilla tends to be more common due to its versatility, I feel like almond extract really takes recipes to a whole new level. It certainly works wonders in these light and fluffy muffins when paired with coconut and chocolate.

YIELD: 10-12 MUFFINS

1½ cup (121 g) rolled oats (quick or old-fashioned)

¼ cup (28 g) almond flour

1½ tsp (6 g) baking powder

1 tsp baking soda

¼ tsp salt

3 large eggs

½ cup (118 ml) unsweetened almond milk

6 tbsp (96 g) almond butter

½ cup (100 g) coconut palm sugar

½ tsp almond extract

½ cup (90 g) semisweet chocolate chips (*for dairy-free, use vegan chocolate chips)

½ cup (38 g) unsweetened coconut, flaked or shredded

¼ cup (25 g) sliced blanched almonds, for topping

Preheat your oven to 350°F (177°C) and prepare a muffin pan by lining the cavities with parchment paper liners. Set aside.

Add the oats, almond flour, baking powder, baking soda and salt to a high-speed blender, and process on high for about 10 seconds or until the oats have broken down into the consistency of a fine flour.

Add the eggs, almond milk, almond butter, coconut palm sugar and almond extract, and process on high for about 30 seconds or until the batter becomes smooth and creamy. Periodically stop and scrape down the sides of your blender, if necessary. Finally, fold in the chocolate chips and coconut by hand.

Spoon the batter into the prepared muffin cups, filling each one about ¾ of the way full. Sprinkle the tops with the almond slices, and more chocolate chips and coconut flakes if desired.

Bake for 17-19 minutes, until the tops of your muffins begin to turn golden brown and a toothpick inserted into the center comes out clean. Allow the muffins to cool in the pan for 10 minutes before transferring them to a wire rack to cool completely. As soon as they've cooled, transfer them to an airtight container and store them at room temperature for up to 5 days, or freeze for up to 3 months.

NOTE

For best results, use a finely ground almond flour made from blanched almonds.

Banana Pecan Crumble Muffins

GLUTEN-FREE, DAIRY-FREE

While the banana muffin base is delicious in its own right, it's really the sweet and crunchy pecan topping that takes these muffins over the top. You can easily replace the pecans with another nut if you don't have them on hand, but you definitely don't want to miss out on this flavor explosion.

YIELD: 10-12 MUFFINS

FOR THE MUFFINS

1½ cups (121 g) rolled oats (quick or old-fashioned)

3 tbsp (21 g) ground flaxseed

½ tsp ground cinnamon

1½ tsp (6 g) baking powder

½ tsp baking soda

¼ tsp salt

2 large eggs

¼ cup (59 ml) unsweetened almond milk

¼ cup (64 g) almond butter

¼ cup (85 g) honey

1 tsp vanilla extract

2 medium-sized ripe bananas, mashed (about 1 cup [200 g])

FOR THE PECAN TOPPING

¼ cup (50 g) coconut palm sugar

2 tbsp (12 g) almond flour

2 tbsp (30 ml) coconut oil, melted

2 tbsp (10 g) old-fashioned rolled oats

½ cup (60 g) chopped pecans

Preheat your oven to 350°F (177°C) and prepare a muffin pan by lining the cavities with parchment paper liners. Set aside.

Add the oats, ground flaxseed, cinnamon, baking powder, baking soda and salt to a high-speed blender, and process on high for about 10 seconds or until the oats have broken down into the consistency of a fine flour.

Add all of the remaining muffin ingredients except for the bananas, and process on high for about 30 seconds or until the batter becomes smooth and creamy. Periodically stop and scrape down the sides of your blender, if necessary. Finally, fold in the mashed bananas by hand.

Spoon the batter into the prepared muffin cups, filling each one about ¾ of the way full. Prepare the pecan topping by combining the sugar, flour and oil in a small bowl. Stir in the oats and pecans. Divide the topping evenly among all the muffins.

Bake for 24-26 minutes, until the tops of your muffins begin to turn golden brown and a toothpick inserted into the center comes out clean. Allow the muffins to cool in the pan for 10 minutes before transferring them to a wire rack to cool completely. As soon as they've cooled, transfer them to an airtight container and store them at room temperature for up to 5 days, or freeze for up to 3 months.

NOTE

You could also use brown sugar instead of coconut palm sugar.

Marbled Banana Chocolate Greek Yogurt Muffins

GLUTEN-FREE, OIL-FREE

These muffins are a variation of my much-loved Banana Oat Greek Yogurt Muffins (page 41) from the Breakfast Muffins chapter. While they may look like they'd be a lot more complicated to make, both the banana and chocolate portions are made from one batter that's whipped up in the blender, and a simple layering technique gives them their pretty marbled quality.

YIELD: 10-12 MUFFINS

1 cup (227 g) plain Greek yogurt

2 medium-sized ripe bananas, mashed (about 1 cup [200 g])

2 large eggs

2 cups (161 g) rolled oats (quick or old-fashioned)

¼ cup (50 g) coconut palm sugar

2 tbsp (43 g) honey

2 tsp (10 ml) vanilla extract

1 tsp baking powder

½ tsp baking soda

3 tbsp (15 g) unsweetened cocoa powder

2-3 tbsp (23-34 g) semisweet chocolate chips, for topping (optional)

Preheat your oven to 350°F (177°C) and prepare a muffin pan by lining the cavities with parchment paper liners. Set aside.

Add all of the ingredients except for the baking powder, baking soda, cocoa powder and chocolate chips to a high-speed blender, and process on high for about 30-40 seconds or until the oats have fully broken down and the batter is smooth and creamy. Periodically stop and scrape down the sides of the blender, if necessary. Add the baking powder and baking soda, and continue to process for about another 5 seconds.

Transfer half of the batter to a separate bowl and set it aside. Add the cocoa powder to the batter remaining in your blender, and process for about 10 seconds or until it becomes fully incorporated. Periodically stop and scrape down the sides of your blender, if necessary.

Spoon a small amount of the banana-only batter into each muffin cavity, enough to cover the bottom. Follow this with a spoonful of the chocolate batter, and continue alternating until both batters have been used up and the muffin cavities are about ¾ full. Use a toothpick to gently swirl the batters around and sprinkle the tops with chocolate chips, if desired.

Bake for 20-22 minutes, until a toothpick inserted into the center comes out clean. Allow the muffins to cool in the pan for 10 minutes before transferring them to a wire rack to cool completely. As soon as they've cooled, transfer them to an airtight container and store them at room temperature for up to 5 days, or freeze for up to 3 months.

NOTES

You could also use a flavored Greek yogurt, but this will slightly alter the taste of the finished product.

You could easily sub the coconut palm sugar with brown sugar.

Carrot Cake Muffins

GLUTEN-FREE, OIL-FREE

These plump and tender muffins are a slight step up from the Spiced Carrot Muffins (page 28) found in the Classic Favorites chapter since they come equipped with the full carrot cake experience, which includes the irresistible cream cheese frosting. But instead of being frosted like cupcakes, they have a sweetened cream cheese swirl that complements the subtle spices in these carrot muffins perfectly and helps keep them healthier.

YIELD: 10-12 MUFFINS

FOR THE MUFFINS

1½ cups (121 g) rolled oats (quick or old-fashioned)

3 tbsp (21 g) ground flaxseed

1 tsp ground cinnamon

2 tsp (8 g) baking powder

1 tsp baking soda

¼ tsp salt

2 large eggs

½ cup (118 ml) unsweetened almond milk

6 tbsp (96 g) almond butter

¼ cup (59 ml) maple syrup

1 tsp vanilla extract

1 cup (115 g) shredded carrots

¼ cup (19 g) unsweetened shredded coconut

FOR THE CREAM CHEESE TOPPING

6 oz (170 g) cream cheese, softened

1 egg yolk

¼ cup (48 g) cane or granulated sugar

Preheat your oven to 350°F (177°C) and prepare a muffin pan by lining the cavities with parchment paper liners. Set aside.

Add the oats, ground flaxseed, cinnamon, baking powder, baking soda and salt to a high-speed blender, and process on high for about 10 seconds or until the oats have broken down into the consistency of a fine flour.

Add all of the remaining muffin ingredients except for the carrots and coconut, and process on high for about 30 seconds or until the batter becomes smooth and creamy. Periodically stop and scrape down the sides of your blender, if necessary. Finally, fold in the carrots and coconut by hand.

Spoon the batter into the prepared muffin cups, filling each one about ¾ of the way full. In a medium-sized bowl, beat the cream cheese until it becomes smooth. Add the egg yolk and sugar, and continue beating until all the ingredients are combined. Top each muffin with 1 tablespoon (15 g) of the cream cheese mixture, and use a toothpick to gently swirl it into the batter.

Bake for 22-24 minutes, until the tops of your muffins begin to turn golden brown and a toothpick inserted into the center comes out clean. Allow the muffins to cool in the pan for 10 minutes before transferring them to a wire rack to cool completely. As soon as they've cooled, transfer them to an airtight container and store them at room temperature for up to 5 days, or freeze for up to 3 months.

Chocolate Lovers' Muffins

This one is for all my fellow chocoholics who understand the need for a chapter devoted to anything and everything chocolate. From the light and fluffy Chocolate Hazelnut Stuffed Muffins stuffed with a luxurious chocolate hazelnut filling (page 90) to the tender Chocolate Cheesecake Muffins accented with a delicious cheesecake swirl (page 98), the muffins in this chapter are here to satisfy your cocoa cravings in the absolute best way possible, especially since they make such a healthy indulgence.

With the exception of the Chocolate Banana Swirl Muffins (page 93) and the Double Chocolate Chip Streusel Muffins (page 105), all of these recipes are grain-free and their textures vary from light and fluffy to dense and fudgy. I tried to use both dark chocolate chunks and semisweet chocolate chips, but you can definitely use them interchangeably depending on how intense of a chocolate flavor you prefer.

Chocolate Cherry Muffins

GLUTEN-FREE, GRAIN-FREE, OIL-FREE, DAIRY-FREE, REFINED SUGAR-FREE

Growing up, my mom would often make a Black Forest cake for birthdays, holidays and special occasions, and I think that's what made me associate the chocolate and cherry combination with happy times. But even without that association, it's hard to deny that chocolate and cherries were made for each other, and the combination is showcased perfectly in these incredibly moist and tender grain-free muffins.

YIELD: 10-12 MUFFINS

1 cup (112 g) almond flour

½ cup (40 g) unsweetened cocoa powder

2 tbsp (14 g) ground flaxseed

1½ tsp (6 g) baking powder

½ tsp baking soda

¼ tsp salt

2 large eggs

¼ cup (59 ml) unsweetened applesauce

¼ cup (64 g) almond butter

6 tbsp (128 g) honey

1 tbsp (15 ml) vanilla extract

1 cup (140 g) chopped sweet cherries, fresh or frozen

Preheat your oven to 350°F (177°C) and prepare a muffin pan by lining the cavities with parchment paper liners. Set aside.

Add the almond flour, cocoa powder, ground flaxseed, baking powder, baking soda and salt to a high-speed blender and pulse a few times until all the dry ingredients become well combined.

Add all of the remaining ingredients except for the cherries, and process on high for about 30 seconds or until the batter becomes smooth and creamy. Periodically stop and scrape down the sides of your blender, as necessary.

Transfer the batter to a medium-sized mixing bowl (this makes it easier to add the cherries), and gently fold in the chopped cherries.

Spoon the batter into the prepared muffin cups, filling each one about ¾ of the way full.

Bake for 25-27 minutes, until a toothpick inserted into the center comes out clean. Allow the muffins to cool in the pan for 10 minutes before transferring them to a wire rack to cool completely. As soon as they've cooled, transfer them to an airtight container and store them at room temperature for up to 5 days, or freeze for up to 3 months.

NOTE

For best results, use a finely ground almond flour made from blanched almonds.

Chocolate Hazelnut Stuffed Muffins

GLUTEN-FREE, GRAIN-FREE, OIL-FREE

While they may look simple at first glance, these rich chocolate muffins house a luxurious hazelnut center that adds a bit of sweet and creamy nuttiness to every bite. For even more hazelnut flavor, melt a bit of the hazelnut spread in the microwave and drizzle it over the tops of the muffins just prior to eating.

YIELD: 10-12 MUFFINS

1 cup (112 g) almond flour

½ cup (40 g) unsweetened cocoa powder

2 tbsp (14 g) ground flaxseed

1½ tsp (6 g) baking powder

½ tsp baking soda

¼ tsp salt

2 large eggs

¼ cup (59 ml) unsweetened applesauce

¼ cup (64 g) almond butter

6 tbsp (128 g) honey

1 tbsp (15 ml) vanilla extract

¼ cup (64 g) chocolate hazelnut spread, such as Nutella

Preheat your oven to 350°F (177°C) and prepare a muffin pan by lining the cavities with parchment paper liners. Set aside.

Add the almond flour, cocoa powder, ground flaxseed, baking powder, baking soda and salt to a high-speed blender and pulse a few times until all the dry ingredients become well combined.

Add all of the remaining ingredients except for the chocolate hazelnut spread, and process on high for about 30 seconds or until the batter becomes smooth and creamy. Periodically stop and scrape down the sides of your blender, as necessary.

Spoon the batter into the prepared muffin cups, filling each one about ⅓ of the way full. Drop 1 teaspoon of chocolate hazelnut spread into the center of each cavity, and then cover with the remaining batter.

Bake for 18–20 minutes, until a toothpick inserted into the center comes out clean. Keep in mind that the chocolate hazelnut spread in the middle means that the toothpick won't come out 100 percent clean, but you'll be able to tell if it's the spread or the batter. And for this recipe, you'll want the toothpick to come out clean of batter! Allow the muffins to cool in the pan for 10 minutes before transferring them to a wire rack to cool completely. As soon as they've cooled, transfer them to an airtight container and store them at room temperature for up to 5 days, or freeze for up to 3 months.

NOTES

For best results, use a finely ground almond flour made from blanched almonds.

Chocolate Banana Swirl Muffins

GLUTEN-FREE, OIL-FREE, DAIRY-FREE, REFINED SUGAR-FREE

Chocolate or banana? Banana or chocolate? If you're as bad at decision making as I am, then these muffins will be your best friends as they allow you to enjoy the best of both worlds in one soft and tender package. And the best part is that, for how impressive they look, they're actually super easy to make and will fit perfectly into your healthy diet.

YIELD: 10-12 MUFFINS

1¼ cups (101 g) rolled oats (quick or old-fashioned)

3 tbsp (21 g) ground flaxseed

2 tsp (8 g) baking powder

1 tsp baking soda

¼ tsp salt

2 large eggs

½ cup (118 ml) unsweetened almond milk

6 tbsp (96 g) almond butter

6 tbsp (128 g) honey

1 tbsp (15 ml) vanilla extract

2 medium-sized ripe bananas, mashed (about 1 cup [200 g])

6 tbsp (30 g) unsweetened cocoa powder

Preheat your oven to 350°F (177°C) and prepare a muffin pan by lining the cavities with parchment paper liners. Set aside.

Add the oats, ground flaxseed, baking powder, baking soda and salt to a high-speed blender, and process on high for about 10 seconds or until the oats have broken down into the consistency of a fine flour.

Add all of the remaining ingredients except for the mashed bananas and cocoa powder, and process on high for about 30 seconds or until the batter becomes smooth and creamy. Periodically stop and scrape down the sides of your blender, if necessary. Fold in the mashed bananas by hand.

Transfer half of the batter to a separate bowl and set it aside. Add the cocoa powder to the batter remaining in your blender, and process for about 10 seconds or until it becomes fully incorporated. Periodically stop and scrape down the sides of your blender, if necessary.

Spoon a small amount of the banana batter into each muffin cavity, enough to cover the bottom. Follow this with a spoonful of the chocolate batter, and continue alternating until both batters have been used up and the muffin cavities are about ¾ full. Use a toothpick to gently swirl the batters around.

Bake for 18-20 minutes, until a toothpick inserted into the center comes out clean. Allow the muffins to cool in the baking pan for 5 minutes before transferring them to a wire rack to cool completely. As soon as they've cooled, transfer them to an airtight container and store them at room temperature for up to 5 days, or freeze for up to 3 months.

Double Chocolate Zucchini Muffins

GLUTEN-FREE, GRAIN-FREE, OIL-FREE, DAIRY-FREE OPTION*

"Zucchini is a miracle worker." Those are five words I never thought I'd utter, but exactly the ones that came out of my mouth after I had my first bite of these ultra-rich chocolate muffins. Not only does the zucchini add a lot of moisture without the need for any extra fat, but you can also sneak some extra veggies into your diet without being able to taste them at all!

YIELD: 10–12 MUFFINS

½ cup + 2 tbsp (50 g) unsweetened cocoa powder

3 tbsp (21 g) ground flaxseed

2 tsp (8 g) baking powder

1 tsp baking soda

¼ tsp salt

3 large eggs

¼ cup (59 ml) unsweetened applesauce

½ cup (128 g) almond butter

6 tbsp (128 g) honey

1 tbsp (15 ml) vanilla extract

1 cup (115 g) grated zucchini, squeezed of excess liquid

½ cup (90 g) semisweet chocolate chips (*for dairy-free, use vegan chocolate chips)

Preheat your oven to 350°F (177°C) and prepare a muffin pan by lining the cavities with parchment paper liners. Set aside.

Add the cocoa powder, ground flaxseed, baking powder, baking soda and salt to a high-speed blender and pulse a few times until all the dry ingredients become well combined.

Add all of the remaining ingredients except for the zucchini and chocolate chips, and process on high for about 30 seconds or until the batter becomes smooth and creamy. Periodically stop and scrape down the sides of your blender, as necessary. Finally, fold in the zucchini and chocolate chips by hand.

Spoon the batter into the prepared muffin cups, filling each one about ¾ of the way full. Sprinkle the tops with additional chocolate chips, if desired.

Bake for 17–19 minutes, until a toothpick inserted into the center comes out clean. Allow the muffins to cool in the pan for 10 minutes before transferring them to a wire rack to cool completely. As soon as they've cooled, transfer them to an airtight container and store them at room temperature for up to 5 days, or freeze for up to 3 months.

NOTE

I like to place the shredded zucchini between two paper towels and squeeze it over the sink. This drains it of just the right amount of liquid to allow the muffin to cook properly.

Dark Chocolate Raspberry Muffins

GLUTEN-FREE, GRAIN-FREE, OIL-FREE, DAIRY-FREE, REFINED SUGAR-FREE

The mouth-watering combination of sweetly tart raspberries and a rich dark chocolate creates a muffin that's flavorful, fudgy and completely irresistible . . . but still deliciously healthy! My taste testers referred to these as "absolutely perfect," but I definitely encourage you to make a batch and see for yourself!

YIELD: 10–12 MUFFINS

1 cup (112 g) almond flour

½ cup (40 g) unsweetened cocoa powder

2 tbsp (14 g) ground flaxseed

1½ tsp (6 g) baking powder

½ tsp baking soda

¼ tsp salt

2 large eggs

¼ cup (59 ml) unsweetened applesauce

¼ cup (64 g) almond butter

6 tbsp (128 g) honey

1 tbsp (15 ml) vanilla extract

1 cup (140 g) raspberries, fresh or frozen

½ cup (90 g) dark chocolate, roughly chopped

Preheat your oven to 350°F (177°C) and prepare a muffin pan by lining the cavities with parchment paper liners. Set aside.

Add the almond flour, cocoa powder, ground flaxseed, baking powder, baking soda and salt to a high-speed blender and pulse a few times until all the dry ingredients become well combined.

Add all of the remaining ingredients except for the raspberries and chocolate chunks, and process on high for about 30 seconds or until the batter becomes smooth and creamy. Periodically stop and scrape down the sides of your blender, as necessary.

Transfer the batter to a medium-sized mixing bowl (this makes it easier to add the mix-ins), and gently fold in the raspberries and chocolate chunks.

Spoon the batter into the prepared muffin cups, filling each one about ¾ of the way full.

Bake for 24–26 minutes, until a toothpick inserted into the center comes out clean. Allow the muffins to cool in the pan for 10 minutes before transferring them to a wire rack to cool completely. As soon as they've cooled, transfer them to an airtight container and store them at room temperature for up to 5 days, or freeze for up to 3 months.

NOTE

For best results, use a finely ground almond flour made from blanched almonds.

Chocolate Cheesecake Muffins

GLUTEN-FREE, GRAIN-FREE, OIL-FREE

To say these disappear quickly is an understatement. I actually had to make several batches of these while doing the recipe development for this book, not because they needed more testing, but because people kept requesting them! It's not hard to see why, though. A light and tender chocolate muffin accented with a sweet and creamy cream cheese swirl makes these pretty irresistible . . . especially because they're such a wonderfully healthy indulgence.

YIELD: 10-12 MUFFINS

FOR THE MUFFINS

¾ cup (84 g) almond flour

½ cup (40 g) unsweetened cocoa powder

2 tbsp (14 g) ground flaxseed

1½ tsp (6 g) baking powder

½ tsp baking soda

¼ tsp salt

2 large eggs

¼ cup (59 ml) unsweetened applesauce

¼ cup (64 g) almond butter

½ cup (170 g) honey

1 tbsp (15 ml) vanilla extract

FOR THE CHEESECAKE SWIRL

6 oz (170 g) cream cheese, softened

1 egg yolk

¼ cup (48 g) cane or granulated sugar

Preheat your oven to 350°F (177°C) and prepare a muffin pan by lining the cavities with parchment paper liners. Set aside.

Add the almond flour, cocoa powder, ground flaxseed, baking powder, baking soda and salt to a high-speed blender and pulse a few times until all the dry ingredients become well combined.

Add all of the remaining muffin ingredients, and process on high for about 30 seconds until the batter becomes smooth and creamy. Periodically stop and scrape down the sides of your blender, as necessary.

Spoon the batter into the prepared muffin cups, filling each one about ⅔ of the way full. In a medium-sized bowl, beat the cream cheese until it becomes smooth. Add the egg yolk and sugar, and continue beating until all the ingredients become well combined. Top each muffin with one tablespoon (15 g) of the cream cheese mixture, and use a toothpick to gently swirl it into the batter.

Bake for 19-21 minutes, until a toothpick inserted into the center comes out clean. Allow the muffins to cool in the pan for 10 minutes before transferring them to a wire rack to cool completely. As soon as they've cooled, transfer them to an airtight container and store them at room temperature for up to 5 days, or freeze for up to 3 months.

Chocolate Ricotta Muffins

GLUTEN-FREE, GRAIN-FREE, OIL-FREE, REFINED SUGAR-FREE

Super moist and chocolaty, these healthy muffins have a slightly denser and fudgier texture that's almost like that of a brownie thanks to the ricotta. Try storing them in the fridge to see how you like them chilled, and feel free to add ½ cup (90 g) of chocolate chips to intensify the chocolate flavor even more.

YIELD: 10–12 MUFFINS

½ cup + 2 tbsp (50 g) unsweetened cocoa powder

2 tbsp (14 g) ground flaxseed

2 tsp (8 g) baking powder

1 tsp baking soda

¼ tsp salt

2 large eggs

6 tbsp (96 g) almond butter

6 tbsp (128 g) honey

2 tsp (10 ml) vanilla extract

¾ cup (165 g) ricotta cheese (regular or light)

Preheat your oven to 350°F (177°C) and prepare a muffin pan by lining the cavities with parchment paper liners. Set aside.

Add all of the ingredients except for the ricotta to a high-speed blender, and process on high for about 30–40 seconds or until the batter becomes smooth and creamy. Periodically stop and scrape down the sides of your blender, as necessary. Finally, fold in the ricotta by hand.

Spoon the batter into the prepared muffin cups, filling each one about ¾ of the way full.

Bake for 21–23 minutes, until a toothpick inserted into the center comes out clean. Allow the muffins to cool in the pan for 10 minutes before transferring them to a wire rack to cool completely. As soon as they've cooled, transfer them to an airtight container and store them at room temperature for up to 5 days, or freeze for up to 3 months.

Mocha Muffins

GLUTEN-FREE, GRAIN-FREE, OIL-FREE, REFINED SUGAR-FREE, DAIRY-FREE OPTION*

Coffee fans will love the subtle espresso undertones in these healthy chocolate muffins—they're perfect alongside your morning cup or as an afternoon pick-me-up. I've paired the espresso with dark chocolate for an even deeper and more intense flavor profile, but you can easily replace the dark chocolate chunks with semisweet chocolate chips if you like your chocolate a little sweeter.

YIELD: 10-12 MUFFINS

1 cup (112 g) almond flour

¼ cup (20 g) unsweetened cocoa powder

3 tbsp (12 g) instant espresso powder

2 tbsp (14 g) ground flaxseed

1½ tsp (6 g) baking powder

½ tsp baking soda

¼ tsp salt

2 large eggs

¼ cup (59 ml) unsweetened applesauce

¼ cup (64 g) almond butter

6 tbsp (128 g) honey

1 tbsp (15 ml) vanilla extract

½ cup (90 g) coarsely chopped dark chocolate chunks (*for dairy-free, use vegan chocolate chips)

Preheat your oven to 350°F (177°C) and prepare a muffin pan by lining the cavities with parchment paper liners. Set aside.

Add the almond flour, cocoa powder, espresso powder, ground flaxseed, baking powder, baking soda and salt to a high-speed blender and pulse a few times until all the dry ingredients become well combined.

Add all of the remaining ingredients except for the chocolate chunks, and process on high for about 30 seconds or until the batter becomes smooth and creamy. Periodically stop and scrape down the sides of your blender, as necessary. Finally, fold in the dark chocolate chunks by hand, saving a few to sprinkle on the tops.

Spoon the batter into the prepared muffin cups, filling each one about ¾ of the way full. Sprinkle the tops with the remaining chocolate chunks.

Bake for 20-22 minutes, until a toothpick inserted into the center comes out clean. Allow the muffins to cool in the pan for 10 minutes before transferring them to a wire rack to cool completely. As soon as they've cooled, transfer them to an airtight container and store them at room temperature for up to 5 days, or freeze for up to 3 months.

NOTE

For best results, use a finely ground almond flour made from blanched almonds.

Double Chocolate Chip Streusel Muffins

GLUTEN-FREE, DAIRY-FREE OPTION*

Unlike regular double chocolate muffins that have the chocolate chips mixed right into the batter, the chocolate in these light and fluffy muffins has been taken out and added to a streusel that gets sprinkled on top for an irresistible dose of chocolate crunchiness in each bite.

YIELD: 10–12 MUFFINS

FOR THE MUFFINS

1 cup (112 g) almond flour

½ cup (40 g) unsweetened cocoa powder

2 tbsp (14 g) ground flaxseed

1½ tsp (6 g) baking powder

½ tsp baking soda

¼ tsp salt

2 large eggs

¼ cup (59 ml) unsweetened applesauce

¼ cup (64 g) almond butter

6 tbsp (128 g) honey

1 tbsp (15 ml) vanilla extract

FOR THE STREUSEL TOPPING

¼ cup (50 g) coconut palm sugar

2 tbsp (12 g) almond flour

2 tbsp (30 ml) coconut oil, melted

2 tbsp (10 g) old-fashioned rolled oats

½ cup (90 g) mini chocolate chips
(*for dairy-free, use vegan chocolate chips)

Preheat your oven to 350°F (177°C) and prepare a muffin pan by lining the cavities with parchment paper liners. Set aside.

Add the almond flour, cocoa powder, ground flaxseed, baking powder, baking soda and salt to a high-speed blender and pulse a few times until all the dry ingredients become well combined.

Add all of the remaining muffin ingredients, and process on high until the batter becomes smooth and creamy, about 30 seconds. Periodically stop and scrape down the sides of your blender, as necessary.

Spoon the batter into the prepared muffin cups, filling each one about ¾ of the way full. Prepare the streusel topping by combining the sugar, flour and coconut oil in a small bowl. Stir in the oats and chocolate chips. Divide the topping evenly among all the muffins.

Bake for 24–26 minutes, until a toothpick inserted into the center comes out clean. Allow the muffins to cool in the pan for 10 minutes before transferring them to a wire rack to cool completely. As soon as they've cooled, transfer them to an airtight container and store them at room temperature for up to 5 days, or freeze for up to 3 months.

Double Chocolate Banana Bread Muffins

GLUTEN-FREE, GRAIN-FREE, OIL-FREE, DAIRY-FREE OPTION*

Chocolate and bananas are a match made in heaven, and these healthy muffins showcase that combination perfectly with lots of fudgy chocolate flavor accented by subtly sweet banana undertones. This recipe also calls for 3 bananas, so it's a great way to use up any ripe ones if you find yourself with too many hanging out on your counter.

YIELD: 10–12 MUFFINS

3 medium-sized ripe bananas, mashed (about 1½ cups [300 g])

3 large eggs

6 tbsp (96 g) almond butter

6 tbsp (128 g) honey

2 tsp (10 ml) vanilla extract

1 tsp apple cider vinegar

¾ cup (60 g) unsweetened cocoa powder

3 tbsp (21 g) coconut flour

1½ tsp (6 g) baking powder

½ tsp baking soda

¼ tsp salt

1 cup (180 g) semisweet chocolate chips (*for dairy-free, use vegan chocolate chips)

Preheat your oven to 350°F (177°C) and prepare a muffin pan by lining the cavities with parchment paper liners. Set aside.

Add the bananas, eggs, almond butter, honey, vanilla and apple cider vinegar to a high-speed blender, and process on high for about 10–15 seconds or until the mixture becomes smooth.

Add all of the remaining ingredients except for the chocolate chips, and continue processing for about 20 seconds or until the dry ingredients become fully incorporated and the batter becomes smooth and creamy. Periodically stop and scrape down the sides of your blender, if necessary.

Spoon the batter into the prepared muffin cups, filling each one about ¾ of the way full. Sprinkle the tops with additional chocolate chips, if desired.

Bake for 17–19 minutes, until a toothpick inserted into the center comes out clean. Allow the muffins to cool in the pan for 10 minutes before transferring them to a wire rack to cool completely. As soon as they've cooled, transfer them to an airtight container and store them at room temperature for up to 5 days, or freeze for up to 3 months.

Single-Serve Minute Muffins

What do you do when you're craving a freshly baked muffin but don't have the 30 or more minutes that it takes to whip up a new batch? Or when you need only a single muffin to satisfy that pesky craving and don't want to have to worry about having leftovers lying around? You whip up one of these healthy single-serve minute muffins!

With just enough batter for a single serving and only 2 minutes of cook time in the microwave, the recipes in this chapter are ready to be enjoyed in less than 5 minutes. You'll find classic flavors like Chocolate Chip Cookie Dough (page 111) and Double Blueberry (page 116), and also those that'll make you feel like you're enjoying a warm slice of Apple Pie (page 127) or a Chocolate Double Raspberry (page 132).

Chocolate Chip Cookie Dough Minute Muffin

GLUTEN-FREE, OIL-FREE, VEGAN OPTION*

It may be one of the simplest flavors there is, but I feel like that's what people love most about it. I remember eating store-bought chocolate chip muffins that were literally the size of my face when I was a little girl, so having a slightly smaller and much healthier version that's just as easy to get my hands on is perfect for when the craving strikes.

YIELD: 1 MUFFIN

3 tbsp (20 g) oat flour

½ tsp baking powder

A pinch of salt

2–3 tbsp (30–44 ml) unsweetened applesauce

1 tbsp (15 ml) maple syrup

½ tbsp (8 g) almond butter

¼ tsp vanilla extract

½ tbsp (6 g) mini chocolate chips (*for vegan option, use vegan chocolate chips)

Combine the oat flour, baking powder and salt in a small microwave-safe mug or bowl.

Add the applesauce, maple syrup, almond butter and vanilla, mixing until all the ingredients are well combined. Fold in the chocolate chips, saving a few to sprinkle on top.

Microwave your muffin on high for 2 minutes and allow it to cool slightly before enjoying.

NOTES

To make your own oat flour, run quick or regular rolled oats through a food processor or blender until they break down into the consistency of a fine flour.

Because flour measurements and microwave strengths can have a little variance, you might have to adjust how much applesauce you add. Start with 2 tablespoons (30 ml) and only add an additional tablespoon (15 ml) if you find your muffin is coming out too dry.

Double Chocolate Brownie Minute Muffin

GLUTEN-FREE, VEGAN OPTION*

This one is for all my fellow chocoholics who know what it's like to get a craving for something rich, moist and chocolaty that needs to be satisfied fast. For an even deeper chocolate taste, replace the chocolate chips with dark chocolate chunks and enjoy the benefit of some added antioxidants.

YIELD: 1 MUFFIN

2 tbsp (13 g) oat flour

1½ tbsp (10 g) unsweetened cocoa powder

½ tsp baking powder

A pinch of salt

3–4 tbsp (44–59 ml) unsweetened applesauce

1 tbsp (15 ml) maple syrup

1½ tsp (7 ml) vegetable oil

½ tbsp (6 g) mini chocolate chips (*for vegan option, use vegan chocolate chips)

Combine the oat flour, cocoa powder, baking powder and salt in a small microwave-safe mug or bowl.

Add all of the remaining ingredients except for the chocolate chips, and mix until well combined. Fold in the chocolate chips, saving a few to sprinkle on top.

Microwave your muffin on high for 2 minutes and allow it to cool slightly before enjoying.

NOTES

To make your own oat flour, run quick or regular rolled oats through a food processor or blender until they break down into the consistency of a fine flour.

Because flour measurements and microwave strengths can have a little variance, you might have to adjust how much applesauce you add. Start with 3 tablespoons (44 ml) and only add an additional tablespoon (15 ml) if you find your muffin is coming out too dry.

Banana Bread Minute Muffin

GLUTEN-FREE, OIL-FREE, VEGAN

I love baking up a fresh loaf of banana bread just as much as anyone else, but there are times where I just can't wait the hour or more that it takes to enjoy a slice. That's when this healthy minute muffin is perfect! You get the delicious taste of banana bread in about 5 minutes from start to finish. And like banana bread, it tastes even better on the second day . . . if you can let it sit for that long.

YIELD: 1 MUFFIN

4 tbsp (27 g) oat flour

½ tsp baking powder

¼ tsp ground cinnamon

A pinch of salt

½ medium-sized ripe banana, mashed (about ¼ cup [57 g])

1–2 tbsp (15–30 ml) unsweetened applesauce

1 tbsp (13 g) coconut palm sugar

1 tbsp (7 g) chopped walnuts (optional)

Combine the oat flour, baking powder, cinnamon and salt in a small microwave-safe mug or bowl.

Add the mashed banana, applesauce and sugar, mixing until all the ingredients are well combined. Fold in the walnut pieces, if using, saving a few to sprinkle on top.

Microwave your muffin on high for 2 minutes and allow it to cool slightly before enjoying.

NOTES

To make your own oat flour, run quick or regular rolled oats through a food processor or blender until they break down into the consistency of a fine flour.

Because flour measurements and microwave strengths can have a little variance, you might have to adjust how much applesauce you add. Start with 1 tablespoon (15 ml) and only add an additional tablespoon (15 ml) if you find your muffin is coming out too dry.

Double Blueberry Minute Muffin

GLUTEN–FREE, VEGAN, REFINED SUGAR–FREE OPTION*

A double dose of berries makes this healthy two-minute muffin both super moist and super flavorful. You can even swap the blueberries with any other berry that you love for a little extra flavor variety! Or try different combinations of berries and jam flavors for something completely new.

YIELD: 1 MUFFIN

3 tbsp (20 g) oat flour

1 tbsp (6 g) blanched almond flour

½ tsp baking powder

A pinch of salt

1–2 tbsp (15–30 ml) unsweetened applesauce

1 tbsp (15 ml) maple syrup

1 tsp vegetable oil

Scant ⅛ tsp almond extract

¼ cup (35 g) fresh blueberries

1–2 tsp (5–10 ml) blueberry jam (*for refined sugar–free, use a jam that's naturally sweetened with fruit juice)

Combine the oat flour, almond flour, baking powder and salt in a small microwave-safe mug or bowl.

Add the applesauce, maple syrup, oil and almond extract, mixing until the ingredients are well combined. Gently fold in the blueberries and drop the jam on top, using a toothpick or knife to swirl it around a little.

Microwave your muffin on high for 2 minutes and allow it to cool slightly before enjoying.

NOTES

To make your own oat flour, run quick or regular rolled oats through a food processor or blender until they break down into the consistency of a fine flour.

If you don't have almond extract, use ¼ teaspoon of vanilla extract.

Because flour measurements and microwave strengths can have a little variance, you might have to adjust how much applesauce you add. Start with 1 tablespoon (15 ml) and only add an additional tablespoon (15 ml) if you find your muffin is coming out too dry.

Snickerdoodle Minute Muffin

GLUTEN-FREE, OIL-FREE, VEGAN

I could have just as easily called this a cinnamon sugar microwave muffin, but I couldn't resist an excuse to say the word "snickerdoodle." Either way, there's nothing more comforting than the classic taste of cinnamon and sugar. Except maybe the classic taste of cinnamon and sugar in a light and fluffy muffin that comes together in 5 minutes from start to finish and makes a perfectly healthy indulgence.

YIELD: 1 MUFFIN

3 tsp (12 g) coconut palm sugar, divided

¼ tsp ground cinnamon

3 tbsp (20 g) oat flour

1 tbsp (6 g) blanched almond flour

½ tsp baking powder

¼ tsp ground cinnamon

A pinch of salt

2-3 tbsp (30-44 ml) unsweetened applesauce

Combine 1 teaspoon of coconut palm sugar and cinnamon in a small bowl. Set aside.

In a separate small mixing bowl, combine the oat flour, almond flour, remaining coconut palm sugar, baking powder, cinnamon and salt. Add the applesauce and mix until all the ingredients are well combined.

Sprinkle a little bit of the cinnamon sugar mixture into the bottom of a small microwave-safe mug or bowl. Add half of the muffin batter, and then sprinkle in more cinnamon sugar. Add the remaining batter, and top with the rest of the cinnamon sugar.

Microwave your muffin on high for 2 minutes and allow it to cool slightly before enjoying.

NOTES

You could also use brown or cane sugar in place of the coconut palm sugar.

To make your own oat flour, run quick or regular rolled oats through a food processor or blender until they break down into the consistency of a fine flour.

Because flour measurements and microwave strengths can have a little variance, you might have to adjust how much applesauce you add. Start with 2 tablespoons (30 ml) and only add an additional tablespoon (15 ml) if you find your muffin is coming out too dry.

Zucchini Minute Muffin

GLUTEN–FREE, OIL–FREE, REFINED SUGAR–FREE OPTION*, VEGAN OPTION*

It's hard to believe there was ever a time where I found the idea of baking with zucchini a bit strange. Not only is it such a great way to add moisture to baked goods without the need for any extra fat from butter or oil, but you also get to sneak some extra veggies into your diet without really being able to detect them at all.

YIELD: 1 MUFFIN

3 tbsp (20 g) oat flour

½ tsp baking powder

Scant ⅛ tsp ground cinnamon

A pinch of salt

1–2 tbsp (15–30 ml) unsweetened applesauce

1 tbsp (15 ml) maple syrup

¼ tsp vanilla extract

¼ cup (29 g) shredded zucchini, squeezed of excess liquid

½ tbsp (6 g) mini chocolate chips (optional, *for refined sugar–free leave them out, and for vegan option use vegan chocolate chips)

Combine the oat flour, baking powder, cinnamon and salt in a small microwave-safe mug or bowl.

Add the applesauce, maple syrup and vanilla, mixing until the ingredients are well combined. Fold in the shredded zucchini and chocolate chips (if using), saving a few to sprinkle on top.

Microwave your muffin on high for 2 minutes and allow it to cool slightly before enjoying.

NOTES

To make your own oat flour, run quick or regular rolled oats through a food processor or blender until they break down into the consistency of a fine flour.

Because flour measurements and microwave strengths can have a little variance, you might have to adjust how much applesauce you add. Start with 1 tablespoon (15 ml) and only add an additional tablespoon (15 ml) if you find your muffin is coming out too dry.

I like to place the shredded zucchini between two paper towels and squeeze it over the sink. This drains it of just the right amount of liquid to allow the muffin to cook properly.

Chocolate Zucchini Minute Muffin

GLUTEN-FREE, OIL-FREE, REFINED SUGAR-FREE, VEGAN

What's the best thing about this minute muffin? It's such a quick and healthy way to satisfy a chocolate craving while not tasting overly healthy at all. If you want to intensify the chocolate flavor even more, add a sprinkle of chocolate chips or dark chocolate chunks to the top before cooking.

YIELD: 1 MUFFIN

2 tbsp (13 g) oat flour

2 tbsp (10 g) unsweetened cocoa powder

½ tsp baking powder

A pinch of salt

2-3 tbsp (30-44 ml) unsweetened applesauce

1 tbsp (15 ml) maple syrup

½ tsp vanilla extract

¼ cup (29 g) shredded zucchini, squeezed of excess liquid

Combine the oat flour, cocoa powder, baking powder and salt in a small microwave-safe mug or bowl.

Add all of the remaining ingredients except for the shredded zucchini, and mix until well combined. Finally, fold in the shredded zucchini.

Microwave your muffin on high for 2 minutes and allow it to cool slightly before enjoying.

NOTES

To make your own oat flour, run quick or regular rolled oats through a food processor or blender until they break down into the consistency of a fine flour.

Because flour measurements and microwave strengths can have a little variance, you might have to adjust how much applesauce you add. Start with 2 tablespoons (30 ml) and only add an additional tablespoon (15 ml) if you find your mug cake is coming out too dry.

I like to place the shredded zucchini between two paper towels and squeeze it over the sink. This drains it of just the right amount of liquid to allow the muffin to cook properly.

Almond Joy Minute Muffin

GLUTEN-FREE, OIL-FREE, VEGAN OPTION*

As delicious as it is, you really want to make sure you don't add too much almond extract to this healthy muffin, as its strong flavor can go from "good" to "overwhelming" quite easily. And as tempting as it is to go all out with the chocolate chips, you really need only a few, as you don't want them to overwhelm the subtler flavors of the almond and coconut.

YIELD: 1 MUFFIN

3 tbsp (20 g) oat flour

1 tbsp (6 g) almond flour

1 tbsp (5 g) unsweetened shredded coconut, plus more for topping

1 tbsp (7 g) sliced almonds, plus more for topping

½ tsp baking powder

A pinch of salt

2–3 tbsp (30–44 ml) unsweetened applesauce

1 tbsp (15 ml) maple syrup

Scant ⅛ tsp almond extract

A few mini chocolate chips, for topping (*for vegan option, use vegan chocolate chips)

Combine the oat flour, almond flour, shredded coconut, sliced almonds, baking powder and salt in a small microwave-safe mug or bowl.

Add the applesauce, maple syrup and almond extract, mixing until the ingredients are well combined. Sprinkle the top with additional almonds and coconut, plus a few chocolate chips, to taste.

Microwave your muffin on high for 2 minutes and allow it to cool slightly before enjoying.

NOTES

To make your own oat flour, run quick or regular rolled oats through a food processor or blender until they break down into the consistency of a fine flour.

Because flour measurements and microwave strengths can have a little variance, you might have to adjust how much applesauce you add. Start with 2 tablespoons (30 ml) and only add an additional tablespoon (15 ml) if you find your muffin is coming out too dry.

If you don't have almond extract, use ¼ teaspoon of vanilla extract.

Apple Pie Minute Muffin

GLUTEN-FREE, OIL-FREE, VEGAN

While traditional apple pie is absolutely delicious, the process of making it can be a little too time consuming and complicated for a lot of people. This single-serve muffin takes about 5 minutes from start to finish, and offers the same nostalgic taste as a freshly baked slice of pie. It also has considerably less sugar and fat, meaning you can enjoy it with a scoop of vanilla ice cream for a healthy indulgence.

YIELD: 1 MUFFIN

3 tbsp (20 g) oat flour

1 tbsp (6 g) blanched almond flour

2 tsp (8 g) coconut palm sugar

½ tsp baking powder

¼ tsp ground cinnamon

A pinch of ground nutmeg

A pinch of salt

2½-3 tbsp (37-44 ml) unsweetened applesauce

¼ tsp vanilla extract

¼ cup (30 g) shredded apple, lightly squeezed of excess juice

Combine the oat flour, almond flour, coconut palm sugar, baking powder, cinnamon, nutmeg and salt in a small microwave-safe mug or bowl.

Add the applesauce and vanilla extract, mixing until the ingredients are well combined. Gently fold in the shredded apple.

Microwave your muffin on high for 2 minutes and allow it to cool slightly before enjoying.

NOTES

To make your own oat flour, run quick or regular rolled oats through a food processor or blender until they break down into the consistency of a fine flour.

You could also use brown or cane sugar instead of the coconut palm sugar.

Because flour measurements and microwave strengths can have a little variance, you might have to adjust how much applesauce you add. Start with 2½ tablespoons (37 ml) and only add an additional tablespoon (15 ml) if you find your muffin is coming out too dry.

I like to place a handful of shredded apple between two paper towels and lightly squeeze it over the sink. This drains it of just the right amount of juice to allow the muffins to cook properly.

Carrot Cake Minute Muffin

GLUTEN-FREE, OIL-FREE, REFINED SUGAR-FREE, VEGAN OPTION*

Carrot Cake is the one instance where I'll choose frosting over cake, which is why I wanted to include a simple cream cheese frosting in this minute muffin. The result is a single-serve carrot cake that feels like an indulgent treat but is actually quite healthy.

YIELD: 1 MUFFIN

FOR THE MUFFIN

3 tbsp (20 g) oat flour

½ tsp baking powder

¼ tsp ground cinnamon

Scant ⅛ tsp ground nutmeg

A pinch of salt

1–2 tbsp (15–30 ml) unsweetened applesauce

1 tbsp (15 ml) maple syrup

¼ tsp vanilla extract

¼ cup (30 g) grated carrot

1 tbsp (7 g) crushed walnuts

FOR THE FILLING

1–2 tbsp (15–30 g) cream cheese (*for vegan option, use non-dairy cream cheese)

½ tsp maple syrup

Combine the oat flour, baking powder, cinnamon, nutmeg and salt in a small microwave-safe mug or bowl.

Add the applesauce, maple syrup and vanilla, mixing until all the ingredients are well combined. Fold in the grated carrot and crushed walnuts, saving a few pieces to sprinkle on top.

Microwave your muffin on high for 2 minutes, then allow it to cool.

Meanwhile, combine the filling ingredients in a small bowl. When the muffin is cool, slice it in half horizontally and spread the filling in the middle.

NOTES

To make your own oat flour, run quick or regular rolled oats through a food processor or blender until they break down into the consistency of a fine flour.

Because flour measurements and microwave strengths can have a little variance, you might have to adjust how much applesauce you add. Start with 1 tablespoon (15 ml) and only add an additional tablespoon (15 ml) if you find your muffin is coming out too dry.

Pumpkin Spice Minute Muffin

GLUTEN-FREE, OIL-FREE, VEGAN OPTION*

While it's definitely more popular in the fall months, I like to keep a can of pumpkin in my pantry all year long just because of how big of a nutritional powerhouse it is. Loaded with fiber and vitamin A, it makes a great low-calorie substitute for butter or oil in baking. Just make sure to use regular canned pumpkin instead of pumpkin pie mix!

YIELD: 1 MUFFIN

4 tbsp (27 g) oat flour

½ tsp baking powder

¼ tsp ground cinnamon

¼ tsp ground ginger

A pinch of ground nutmeg

A pinch of salt

3 tbsp (44 g) canned pumpkin puree

1-2 tbsp (15-30 ml) unsweetened
   applesauce

1 tbsp (13 g) coconut palm sugar

½ tbsp (6 g) mini chocolate chips,
   optional (*for vegan option, use
   vegan chocolate chips)

Combine the oat flour, baking powder, cinnamon, ginger, nutmeg and salt in a small microwave-safe mug or bowl.

Add the pumpkin, applesauce and sugar, mixing until all the ingredients are well combined. Fold in the chocolate chips, if using, saving a few to sprinkle on top.

Microwave your muffin on high for 2 minutes and allow it to cool slightly before enjoying.

NOTES

To make your own oat flour, run quick or regular rolled oats through a food processor or blender until they break down into the consistency of a fine flour.

Because flour measurements and microwave strengths can have a little variance, you might have to adjust how much applesauce you add. Start with 1 tablespoon (15 ml) and only add an additional tablespoon (15 ml) if you find your muffin is coming out too dry.

Chocolate Double Raspberry Minute Muffin

GLUTEN-FREE, OIL-FREE, VEGAN, REFINED SUGAR-FREE OPTION*

The sweetly tart taste of raspberries paired with the deeper and earthier taste of chocolate make this healthy minute muffin an absolute joy for the senses. And if you're not big on raspberries or don't have any on hand? Substitute them with strawberries or cherries for an equally delicious treat!

YIELD: 1 MUFFIN

2 tbsp (13 g) oat flour

2 tbsp (10 g) unsweetened cocoa powder

½ tsp baking powder

A pinch of salt

1–2 tbsp (15–30 ml) unsweetened applesauce

1 tbsp (15 ml) maple syrup

½ tsp vanilla extract

¼ cup (35 g) raspberries, fresh or frozen

½ tsp raspberry jam (*for refined sugar-free, use a jam that's been sweetened with fruit juice)

Combine the oat flour, cocoa powder, baking powder and salt in a small microwave-safe mug or bowl.

Add the applesauce, maple syrup and vanilla extract, mixing until all the ingredients are well combined. Gently fold in the raspberries and drop the jam on top, using a toothpick or knife to swirl it around a little.

Microwave your muffin on high for 2 minutes and allow it to cool slightly before enjoying.

NOTES

To make your own oat flour, run quick or regular rolled oats through a food processor or blender until they break down into the consistency of a fine flour.

Because flour measurements and microwave strengths can have a little variance, you might have to adjust how much applesauce you add. Start with 1 tablespoon (15 ml) and only add an additional tablespoon (15 ml) if you find your mug cake is coming out too dry. I found 1½ tablespoons (22 ml) to be perfect.

Healthy Brownies and Snack Bars

And now for something a little different! As wonderful as muffins are, it's always nice to have a few options. Variety is, after all, the spice of life, and that's exactly what you'll find with the recipes in this chapter—a variety of healthy snack bars that you can make when you're in the mood for something other than muffins.

From ridiculously fudgy grain-free Double Chocolate Brownies (page 137) and Soft and Chewy Protein Granola Bars (page 142) that are way better than any of the ones you can get from the store, to quick and easy soft-baked Banana Bread Bars (page 138) or Apple Pie Bars (page 145), each of these recipes is perfect for midday snacking.

Double Chocolate Brownies

GLUTEN-FREE, GRAIN-FREE, DAIRY-FREE OPTION*

Rich, fudgy and fully equipped with those gorgeous crackly tops, these grain-free brownies make a perfect dessert for parties or special occasions as they're guaranteed to please. They're a reader favorite and I had to include them in this book because of the countless rave reviews they received from everyone who's made them as being the best gluten-free brownies they've ever had.

YIELD: 16 BROWNIES

6 tbsp (89 ml) coconut oil

1 cup (180 g) semisweet chocolate chips (*for dairy-free, use vegan chocolate chips)

2 large eggs, room temperature

⅔ cup (133 g) coconut palm sugar

2 tsp (10 ml) vanilla extract

¼ cup (20 g) unsweetened cocoa powder

3 tbsp (21 g) arrowroot powder

¼ tsp salt

Preheat your oven to 350°F (177°C) and prepare an 8 x 8-inch (20.3 x 20.3-cm) baking pan by lining it with a sheet of aluminum foil, leaving a few inches of overhang on the sides to allow for easy removal. Grease the foil with oil or cooking spray and set aside.

Add the coconut oil and chocolate chips to a small saucepan set over low heat. Stir until the oil and chocolate have melted before removing the pan from the heat and setting it aside to cool slightly.

Using a handheld mixer or a stand mixer fitted with the whisk attachment, beat together the eggs, sugar and vanilla extract for about 2 minutes or until the mixture becomes smooth and pale. Add the melted chocolate mixture and mix until well combined. Reduce the speed to low and add the cocoa powder, arrowroot powder and salt, mixing until well combined and scraping down the sides of the bowl as necessary. The batter should be thick and smooth.

Pour the batter into your prepared pan, spreading it evenly with a greased spatula. Bake for 25–30 minutes, until the center is set. Remove from the oven and let the brownies cool in the pan for about 15 minutes before transferring them to a wire rack to cool completely. Store your brownies in an airtight container at room temperature for up to 5 days.

NOTES

You can use granulated sugar in place of the coconut palm sugar.

You can also use cornstarch in place of the arrowroot.

Banana Bread Bars

GLUTEN-FREE, GRAIN-FREE, OIL-FREE, DAIRY-FREE OPTION*

These deliciously healthy bars are perfect for those who want to enjoy the taste of banana bread without having to go through the hour-long process of making it. They're whipped up in the blender in less than 5 minutes, and so tender and fluffy that you'd never guess they were 100 percent grain-free and oil-free!

YIELD: 12-16 BARS

2 medium-sized ripe bananas, mashed (about 1 cup [200 g])

2 large eggs

2 tbsp (32 g) almond butter

6 tbsp (75 g) coconut palm sugar

1 tsp vanilla extract

½ cup (56 g) almond flour

6 tbsp (42 g) coconut flour

1½ tsp (6 g) baking powder

½ cup (90 g) semisweet chocolate chips (*for dairy-free, use vegan chocolate chips)

Preheat your oven to 350°F (177°C) and prepare an 8 x 8-inch (20.3 x 20.3-cm) baking pan by lining it with a sheet of aluminum foil or parchment paper, leaving a few inches of overhang on the sides to allow for easy removal. Lightly grease and set aside.

Add the bananas, eggs, almond butter, sugar and vanilla extract to a high-speed blender, and process on high for about 10 seconds or until all of the ingredients are combined and the mixture is smooth.

Add the almond flour, coconut flour and baking powder, and continue processing for about 30-40 seconds or until the batter becomes smooth and creamy. Finally, fold in the chocolate chips by hand, reserving a couple tablespoons to sprinkle on the top.

Transfer the batter into your prepared pan and use a spatula to distribute it evenly before topping it with the reserved chocolate chips. Bake for 25-27 minutes, until the bars begin to turn golden brown around the edges and a toothpick inserted into the center comes out clean. Remove them from the oven and let them cool in the pan for about 15 minutes before transferring them to a wire rack to cool completely. Use a sharp knife to cut them into individual bars and store them in an airtight container at room temperature for up to 5 days.

NOTE

You can also use brown sugar in place of the coconut palm sugar.

No-Bake Dark Chocolate Coconut Granola Bars

GLUTEN-FREE, VEGAN, REFINED SUGAR-FREE

The combination of chocolate, coconut and nut butter is completely irresistible, which is probably why it's impossible to make a batch of these bars last for more than a few days! I used almond butter because of my allergy to peanuts, but feel free to replace it with peanut butter if that's what you have on hand! They'll be just as soft, chewy and indulgently healthy.

YIELD: 12 BARS

½ cup (160 g) brown rice syrup

½ cup (128 g) almond butter

1 tsp vanilla extract

¼ tsp salt

1 cup (80 g) old-fashioned rolled oats

1 cup (90 g) unsweetened coconut, shredded or flaked

2 tbsp (14 g) coconut flour

½ cup (90 g) vegan dark chocolate chips or chunks

½ tsp coconut oil

Line an 8 x 8-inch (20.3 x 20.3-cm) baking pan with a sheet of aluminum foil or parchment paper, leaving a few inches of overhang on the sides to allow for easy removal. Set aside.

Add the brown rice syrup and almond butter to a medium-sized microwave-safe bowl and heat on high for about 1 minute or until the ingredients are fully melted and combined. Alternatively, you could melt the ingredients on the stovetop in a small saucepan set over medium heat. Add the vanilla and salt, and mix until smooth.

Add the oats, shredded coconut and coconut flour, and mix until everything is fully combined.

Transfer the mixture to the prepared baking pan and use a spatula or your hands to spread it out evenly, making sure to press down firmly. Set aside.

Add the chocolate chunks and coconut oil to a microwave-safe bowl and heat on high for 30-second intervals, mixing between each round. When the chocolate is fully melted and smooth, drizzle it over the top of the bars and use a spatula to spread it out evenly. Sprinkle with additional shredded coconut, if desired.

Cover the pan with a sheet of foil and place it into the fridge or freezer until the chocolate has set.

When the bars have set, remove them from the pan using the foil overhang and use a sharp knife to cut them into 12 individual bars. Store them in an airtight container in the fridge for up to a week.

NOTE

You could also use honey instead of brown rice syrup if you don't need these to be vegan.

Soft and Chewy Protein Granola Bars

GLUTEN-FREE, OIL-FREE, VEGAN OPTION*

I know it's not right to play favorites, but if I had to choose just one favorite recipe from my blog, this would be it. I've easily made them over 100 times since first developing the recipe, and I almost always have some of these bars on hand for a quick and nutritious snack. Everyone I've introduced them to agrees that they're so much better (and less expensive!) than store-bought.

YIELD: 12 BARS

2 cups (161 g) quick oats

½ cup (40 g) vanilla protein powder (*for vegan, use a plant-based protein powder)

2 tbsp (14 g) ground flaxseed

1 tsp ground cinnamon

¼ tsp salt

¼ cup (64 g) almond butter

¼ cup (80 g) brown rice syrup

½ cup (118 ml) unsweetened almond milk

1 tsp vanilla extract

⅓ cup (59 g) mini chocolate chips (*for vegan, use vegan chocolate chips)

Preheat your oven to 350°F (177°C) and prepare an 8 x 8-inch (20.3 x 20.3-cm) baking pan by lining it with a sheet of aluminum foil or parchment paper, leaving a few inches of overhang on the sides to allow for easy removal. Set aside.

In a large mixing bowl, combine the oats, protein powder, ground flaxseed, cinnamon and salt. Set aside.

In a medium-sized mixing bowl, combine the almond butter, brown rice syrup, almond milk and vanilla. Mix until fully combined before pouring into the dry ingredients. Mix until the ingredients are well combined and fold in the chocolate chips.

Transfer the batter into your prepared pan, making sure it's distributed evenly, and press down firmly. Bake for 18–20 minutes, until the center is set and the bars begin to turn golden brown around the edges. Remove from the oven and let them cool in the pan for about 15 minutes before transferring them to a wire rack to cool completely. Use a sharp knife to cut them into individual bars and store them in an airtight container at room temperature for up to 5 days, or in the fridge for up to 2 weeks.

NOTES

I've tried these with several different protein powders (whey, plant-based, etc.) and each one works just fine, so use whichever one is your favorite and meets your dietary needs.

You can also use honey instead of brown rice syrup if you don't need these to be vegan.

Apple Pie Bars

GLUTEN-FREE, OIL-FREE, VEGAN

Growing up, my mom would regularly make us a Polish apple cake called a *szarlotka*, and I honestly couldn't believe how much these bars reminded me of one of my favorite childhood desserts! My version uses considerably less sugar and no butter, oil or eggs, but still has that delicious buttery taste courtesy of the almond flour in the crust.

YIELD: 12–16 BARS

FOR THE CRUST

1 cup (80 g) rolled oats (quick or old-fashioned)

1 cup (128 g) almond flour

½ cup (118 ml) unsweetened applesauce

¼ cup (50 g) coconut palm sugar

¼ tsp salt

FOR THE APPLE TOPPING

2 medium-sized apples, peeled and thinly sliced

¼ cup (50 g) coconut palm sugar

2 tbsp (12 g) almond flour

1 tsp ground cinnamon

Preheat your oven to 350°F (177°C) and prepare an 8 x 8-inch (20.3 x 20.3-cm) baking pan by lining it with a sheet of aluminum foil or parchment paper, leaving a few inches of overhang on the sides to allow for easy removal. Set aside.

Add the oats and almond flour to a high-speed blender or food processor, and process on high for about 10 seconds or until the oats have broken down into the consistency of a fine flour. Add the remaining crust ingredients and continue processing for about 20–30 seconds until it forms into a sticky dough. Make sure to stop and scrape down the sides of your blender/processor, as necessary.

Transfer the dough to your prepared baking pan, using a greased spatula to spread it out evenly. Set aside.

Make the topping by combining all the ingredients in a large mixing bowl and tossing until the apple slices are evenly coated. Layer them over the top of the crust, pressing down and squeezing them in pretty tightly.

Bake for 30–35 minutes, until the apple topping begins to turn golden brown. Remove the bars from the oven and let them cool in the pan for about 15 minutes before transferring them to a wire rack to cool completely. Use a sharp knife to cut them into individual bars and store them in an airtight container at room temperature for up to 5 days.

NOTES

For best results, use a finely ground almond flour made from blanched almonds.

You could also use regular brown or granulated sugar instead of the coconut palm sugar.

You can use whichever apple you like, but I find that a slightly tarter and firmer apple like a Pink Lady gives the best flavor and texture.

Greek Yogurt Brownies

GLUTEN-FREE, OIL-FREE

Fans of slightly cake-like brownies will love this lightened up recipe. It calls for Greek yogurt instead of butter or oil to keep the brownies moist, and a good amount of cocoa powder to make sure that chocolate flavor shines through. You can also add a handful of chocolate chips or nuts to switch things up!

YIELD: 16 BROWNIES

- ½ cup (114 g) plain or vanilla Greek yogurt
- ¼ cup (64 g) almond butter
- 2 large eggs
- ½ cup (40 g) rolled oats (quick or old-fashioned)
- ½ cup (40 g) unsweetened cocoa powder
- ⅔ cup (133 g) coconut palm sugar
- 1 tsp baking powder

Preheat your oven to 350°F (177°C) and prepare an 8 x 8-inch (20.3 x 20.3-cm) baking pan by lining it with a sheet of aluminum foil or parchment paper, leaving a few inches of overhang on the sides to allow for easy removal. Grease with cooking spray and set aside.

Add all of the ingredients to a high-speed blender in the order listed, and process on high for about 1–2 minutes or until the oats have fully broken down and the batter becomes smooth and creamy.

Pour the batter into your prepared baking pan, using a spatula to distribute it evenly. Bake for 25–30 minutes, until a toothpick inserted into the center comes out clean. Remove the brownies from the oven and let them cool in the pan for about 15 minutes before transferring them to a wire rack to cool completely. Store your brownies in an airtight container at room temperature for up to 5 days.

Almond Butter Cookie Bars

GLUTEN–FREE, VEGAN

As much as I love cookies, I know I can't be the only one who doesn't always want to take the time to shape them individually. That's why cookie bars like this are perfect—all the dough gets dumped into a baking pan and out come soft, baked cookie bars! You can use peanut butter in place of almond butter if that's what you have on hand, but the bars will come out tasting differently . . . which shouldn't be a problem for PB lovers!

YIELD: 12–16 BARS

¼ cup (64 g) almond butter

2 tbsp (27 g) coconut oil

¼ cup (50 g) coconut palm sugar

2 tbsp (40 g) brown rice syrup

2 tbsp (30 ml) unsweetened almond milk

¼ tsp almond extract

1 cup (112 g) almond flour

¾ cup (60 g) rolled oats (quick or old-fashioned), ground into a flour

1½ tsp (6 g) baking powder

¼ tsp salt

½ cup (90 g) vegan chocolate chips

Preheat your oven to 350°F (177°C) and prepare an 8 x 8-inch (20.3 x 20.3-cm) baking pan by lining it with a sheet of aluminum foil or parchment paper, leaving a few inches of overhang on the sides to allow for easy removal. Set aside.

Add the almond butter and coconut oil to a microwave-safe bowl and heat on high for about 1 minute or until both ingredients are fully melted and combined. Alternatively, you could melt the ingredients on the stovetop in a small saucepan set over medium heat. Remove from the heat and add the coconut palm sugar, brown rice syrup, almond milk and almond extract, mixing until fully combined. Set aside.

In a large mixing bowl, combine the almond flour, ground oats, baking powder and salt. Add the wet ingredients to the dry ingredients and mix until well combined before folding in the chocolate chips.

Transfer the batter into your prepared pan, making sure it's distributed evenly and pressed down firmly. Bake for 13–15 minutes, until the center is set and the bars begin to turn brown around the edges. Remove from the oven and let them cool in the pan for about 15 minutes before transferring them to a wire rack to cool completely. Use a sharp knife to cut them into individual bars and store them in an airtight container at room temperature for up to 5 days.

NOTES

You can also use brown sugar instead of the coconut palm sugar.

You can also use regular chocolate chips and honey instead of the brown rice syrup if you don't need these to be vegan.

Fudgy Chocolate Crunch Squares

GLUTEN-FREE, OIL-FREE, VEGAN OPTION*

I've always loved Rice Krispies Treats®, and I came to love them even more when I learned that you could make them healthier by replacing the marshmallows with brown rice syrup and the butter with almond butter. Toss some melted chocolate in the mix, and you've got a 4-ingredient chewy and crispy snack bar that's guaranteed to please!

YIELD: 8 SQUARES

¼ **cup (45 g) chocolate chips (*for vegan option, use vegan chocolate chips)**

6 **tbsp (96 g) almond butter**

¼ **cup (80 g) brown rice syrup**

2 **cups (60 g) crispy rice cereal**

Line a 9 x 5-inch (23 x 13-cm) loaf pan with a sheet of aluminum foil or parchment paper, leaving a few inches of overhang on the sides to allow for easy removal. Generously spray the foil with cooking spray and set aside.

Melt the chocolate and almond butter in a small saucepan set over medium-low heat, stirring regularly to prevent burning. Remove the pan from the heat and add the brown rice syrup, stirring until the mixture is smooth. Finally, add the crispy rice cereal and stir to make sure it's well coated.

Transfer the mixture to the prepared loaf pan and use a spatula or your hands to spread it out evenly, making sure to press down firmly. Cover the pan with a sheet of foil and place it into the freezer to set for at least 15 minutes.

When the bars have set, remove them from the pan using the foil overhang and use a sharp knife to cut them into individual squares. Store them in a sealed container in the fridge or freezer for best results.

NOTE

*You could also use honey in place of the brown rice syrup if you don't need these to be vegan.

Pumpkin Spice Bars

GLUTEN-FREE, GRAIN-FREE, OIL-FREE, DAIRY-FREE OPTION*

Light and fluffy, these fall-inspired bars boast a complex flavor profile that combines the earthy taste of pumpkin with the deeper taste of dark chocolate. These flavors are then accented by warming spices such as cinnamon, ginger and nutmeg to create a treat that's as comforting as it is healthy.

YIELD: 12-16 BARS

¾ cup (175 g) canned pumpkin puree

2 large eggs

2 tbsp (32 g) almond butter

6 tbsp (75 g) coconut palm sugar

1 tbsp (15 ml) unsweetened almond milk

2 tsp (5 g) ground cinnamon

1 tsp ground ginger

½ tsp ground nutmeg

½ cup (56 g) almond flour

6 tbsp (42 g) coconut flour

1½ tsp (6 g) baking powder

½ cup (90 g) dark chocolate chunks or chips (*for dairy-free, use vegan dark chocolate)

Preheat your oven to 350°F (177°C) and prepare an 8 x 8-inch (20.3 x 20.3-cm) baking pan by lining it with a sheet of aluminum foil or parchment paper, leaving a few inches of overhang on the sides to allow for easy removal. Lightly grease the foil and set aside.

Add the pumpkin puree, eggs, almond butter, sugar, almond milk, cinnamon, ginger and nutmeg to a high-speed blender, and process on high for about 10 seconds or until all of the ingredients are combined and the mixture is smooth.

Add the almond flour, coconut flour and baking powder, and continue processing for about 30-40 seconds until the batter becomes smooth and creamy. Finally, fold in the chocolate chips by hand, reserving a couple tablespoons to sprinkle on the top. The batter will be a little thick and paste-like, which is normal.

Transfer the batter into your prepared pan and use a spatula to distribute it evenly before topping with the remaining chocolate chips. Bake for 25-27 minutes, until the bars begin to turn golden brown around the edges and a toothpick inserted into the center comes out clean. Remove them from the oven and let them cool in the pan for about 15 minutes before transferring them to a wire rack to cool completely. Use a sharp knife to cut them into individual bars and store them in an airtight container at room temperature for up to 5 days.

NOTE

You can also use brown sugar instead of coconut palm sugar.

No-Bake Dark Chocolate Trail Mix Bars

GLUTEN–FREE, VEGAN, REFINED SUGAR–FREE

Trail mix is my kryptonite, especially when dark chocolate and raisins are involved. I've structured these no-bake bars so that you can customize them based on your favorite trail mix ingredients, so feel free to switch up what kind of seeds and dried fruit you use to create a completely new flavor profile.

YIELD: 12 BARS

½ cup (160 g) brown rice syrup

2 tbsp (32 g) nut or seed butter

1 tbsp (14 g) coconut oil

¾ cup (60 g) old-fashioned rolled oats

1 cup (30 g) crispy rice cereal

½ tsp salt

½ cup (76 g) dried fruit (raisins and cranberries shown here)

½ cup (70 g) pumpkin or sunflower seeds

½ cup (90 g) vegan dark chocolate, melted

Line an 8 x 8-inch (20.3 x 20.3-cm) baking pan with a sheet of aluminum foil or parchment paper, leaving a few inches of overhang on the sides to allow for easy removal. Generously spray with cooking spray and set aside.

Add the brown rice syrup, nut or seed butter and coconut oil to a microwave-safe bowl and heat on high for about 1 minute or until all the ingredients are fully melted and combined. Alternatively, you could melt the ingredients on the stovetop in a small saucepan set over medium-low heat. Be sure not to let the ingredients come to a boil.

Combine all the remaining ingredients except for the melted chocolate in a large mixing bowl, stirring until everything is evenly distributed. Pour the wet ingredients into the dry ingredients and mix well.

Transfer the mixture to the prepared baking pan and use a spatula or your hands to spread it out evenly, making sure to press down firmly. Cover the pan with a sheet of foil and place it into the freezer to set for at least 20 minutes.

When the bars have set, remove them from the pan using the foil overhang and use a sharp knife to cut them into 12 individual bars.

To apply the chocolate coating, begin by lining a large baking sheet with parchment paper. Add the chocolate to a microwave–safe dish and heat on high in 20-second intervals until it is fully melted and combined, about 1–2 minutes. Alternatively, you could use a double boiler method to melt it over the stovetop.

Transfer the melted chocolate to a large shallow bowl, and dip each bar into it, coating just the bottom or rolling it around so that it's completely coated. Place the coated bars on the baking sheet and transfer them to the freezer for about 10 minutes to allow the chocolate to set. Store the bars in a sealed container at room temperature for up to 2 weeks.

NOTE

You could also use honey in place of the brown rice syrup if you don't need these to be vegan.

Date Squares

GLUTEN-FREE, VEGAN

Besides being absolutely delicious, dates bring a lot of health benefits to the table as well. They're packed with fiber and B-vitamins, and are often seen as one of the best dietary sources of potassium there is. And when you add dates to these flourless bars? They're all that in an ooey, gooey filling that's completely irresistible when combined with a soft-baked crust.

YIELD: 16 SQUARES

FOR THE CRUST

1 cup (80 g) rolled oats (quick or old-fashioned)

1 cup (128 g) almond flour

½ cup (118 ml) unsweetened applesauce

2 tbsp (30 ml) coconut oil, melted

2 tbsp (25 g) coconut palm sugar

¼ tsp salt

FOR THE FILLING

1½ cups (227 g) pitted dates

2 tbsp (30 ml) lemon juice (roughly 1 lemon)

½ tsp ground cinnamon

Preheat your oven to 325°F (163°C) and prepare an 8 x 8-inch (20.3 x 20.3-cm) baking pan by lining it with a sheet of aluminum foil or parchment paper, leaving a few inches of overhang on the sides to allow for easy removal. Set aside.

Add the oats and almond flour to a high-speed blender or food processor, and process on high for about 10 seconds or until the oats have broken down into the consistency of a fine flour. Add the remaining crust ingredients and continue processing for about 20–30 seconds until a sticky dough begins to form. Make sure to stop and scrape down the sides of your blender/processor as necessary.

Transfer the dough to a medium-sized bowl, divide it in half and press half into your prepared baking pan, using a greased spatula to spread it out evenly. Set aside.

To make the filling, add all the ingredients to the now empty blender/processor, and process on high until the dates have broken down into a sticky paste. Stop and scrape down the sides of the bowl as needed, and add a splash of water if the mixture is being stubborn.

Transfer the date filling to the baking pan, and use a greased spatula to spread it over the dough layer. Top with the remaining dough by breaking it up into about 6 or 7 chunks, distributing them over the top of the filling, and using your spatula to spread them out.

Bake for 25–30 minutes, until the center is set and the bars begin to turn golden brown around the edges. Remove from the oven and let them cool in the pan for about 15 minutes before transferring them to a wire rack to cool completely. Use a sharp knife to cut them into individual bars and store them in an airtight container at room temperature for up to 5 days.

NOTE

You could also use regular brown or granulated sugar instead of the coconut palm sugar.

Soft & Chewy Flourless Cookies

The earliest baking memories I have involve me hanging out in the kitchen with my mom while she whipped up a batch of chocolate chip oatmeal cookies. I remember sitting by the oven waiting for that moment when we'd sit down together and enjoy one (or two) alongside a cold glass of milk. I feel like everyone has some warm and fuzzy memories involving cookies, which is why I included a chapter dedicated to them. Well, that and I wanted to make sure you had more healthy options to turn to if you weren't in the mood for muffins or bars but still wanted something indulgent-feeling.

The cookies in this chapter include all the classic favorites that we grew up with like Chocolate Chip (page 161), Oatmeal Raisin (page 162) and White Chocolate Macadamia (page 174). Only this time, they're made without any flour, butter or refined sugar. And the best part? They come out just as soft, chewy and delicious as you remember.

Chocolate Chip Cookies

GLUTEN-FREE, GRAIN-FREE, OIL-FREE, DAIRY-FREE OPTION*

These cookies are exactly what a chocolate chip cookie should be: soft, chewy and loaded with chocolate in every bite. They also happen to be 100 percent grain-free and made without any butter. With only one bowl to wash and 5 minutes of hands-on time, they're the perfect, quick and easy answer to those cookie cravings. And if you're a fan of the deeper taste of dark chocolate? Replace the chocolate chips with roughly chopped chunks of dark chocolate.

YIELD: 18-22 COOKIES

1 cup (256 g) almond butter

1 large egg

⅓ cup (78 ml) maple syrup

1 tsp vanilla extract

1 tsp baking soda

1 tbsp (7 g) arrowroot powder

½ cup (90 g) chocolate chips
(*for dairy-free, use vegan chocolate chips)

Preheat your oven to 350°F (177°C) and line a cookie sheet with parchment paper or a non-stick baking mat. Set aside.

In a large mixing bowl, use an electric mixer to beat the almond butter, egg, maple syrup and vanilla until the mixture becomes smooth and creamy, about 1-2 minutes. Add the baking soda and arrowroot powder, and continue beating for about 30 seconds or until both dry ingredients become well incorporated. Finally, fold in the chocolate chips by hand.

Using a rounded tablespoon, drop the dough onto your prepared baking sheet, spacing them about 2 inches (5 cm) apart. Use a paper towel to gently press down on all the cookies to flatten them slightly—this will absorb some of the excess oil from the almond butter. Press a few additional chocolate chips into the tops of the cookies, if desired.

Bake the cookies for 10-12 minutes, until the edges begin to turn golden brown. They'll look a little soft and underbaked at first, but they'll continue to firm up as they cool. Allow the cookies to cool on the baking sheet for about 10 minutes before transferring them to a wire rack to cool completely. As soon as they've cooled, cover them tightly and store them at room temperature for up to 7 days.

NOTES

For best results, use a store-bought, no-stir variety of almond butter because the natural oils could alter the texture.

Cornstarch will also work in place of the arrowroot powder.

Oatmeal Raisin Cookies

GLUTEN-FREE, DAIRY-FREE, REFINED SUGAR-FREE

Don't tell the chocolate chip cookies, but oatmeal raisin cookies may very well be my #1 favorite. They're the first cookie I remember my mom making for me as a child, and the first thing I learned to bake on my own. Unlike those cookies, this healthier version is made without any flour, butter or refined sugar, but they're just as soft, chewy and delicious as the ones I remember from my childhood.

YIELD: 16-20 COOKIES

½ cup (128 g) almond butter

1 large egg

⅓ cup (78 ml) maple syrup

2 tbsp (30 ml) melted coconut oil

1 tsp vanilla extract

1 tbsp (7 g) arrowroot powder

1 tsp ground cinnamon

1 tsp baking soda

1½ cups (121 g) old-fashioned rolled oats

½ cup (76 g) raisins

Preheat your oven to 350°F (177°C) and line a cookie sheet with parchment paper or a non-stick baking mat. Set aside.

In a large mixing bowl, use an electric mixer to beat the almond butter, egg, maple syrup, coconut oil and vanilla for about 1-2 minutes or until the mixture becomes smooth and creamy. Add the arrowroot powder, cinnamon and baking soda, and continue beating for about 30 seconds or until each becomes well incorporated. Finally, fold in the oats and raisins by hand.

Using a rounded tablespoon, drop the dough onto your prepared baking sheet, spacing them about 2 inches (5 cm) apart.

Bake the cookies for 10-12 minutes, until the edges begin to turn golden brown. They'll seem a little soft and underbaked at first, but they'll continue to firm up as they cool. Allow the cookies to cool on the baking sheet for about 10 minutes before transferring them to a wire rack to cool completely. As soon as they've cooled, cover them tightly and store them at room temperature for up to 7 days.

NOTES

For best results, use a store-bought, no-stir variety of almond butter because the natural oils could alter the texture.

Cornstarch will also work in place of the arrowroot powder.

Double Chocolate Brownie Cookies

GLUTEN-FREE, GRAIN-FREE, DAIRY-FREE OPTION*

Slightly crispy on the outside and soft and chewy on the inside, the biggest problem with these extra chocolaty, grain-free cookies is that it's nearly impossible to stop at just one! And while the recipe calls for dark chocolate chunks, feel free to use semisweet chocolate chips if you want a slightly sweeter taste.

YIELD: 12 LARGE COOKIES

¾ cup (192 g) almond butter

1 large egg

⅓ cup (78 ml) maple syrup

2 tbsp (30 ml) melted coconut oil

1 tsp vanilla extract

1 tbsp (7 g) arrowroot powder

1 tsp baking soda

¼ cup (20 g) unsweetened cocoa powder

½ cup (90 g) coarsely chopped dark chocolate chunks (*for dairy-free, use vegan dark chocolate)

Preheat your oven to 350°F (177°C) and line a cookie sheet with parchment paper or a non-stick baking mat. Set aside.

In a large mixing bowl, use an electric mixer to beat the almond butter, egg, maple syrup, coconut oil and vanilla for about 1–2 minutes until the mixture becomes smooth and creamy. Add the arrowroot powder and baking soda, and continue beating for about 30 seconds or until both dry ingredients become well incorporated.

Stir in the cocoa powder by hand (to avoid it flying everywhere), and gently fold in the chocolate chunks.

Using a rounded tablespoon, drop the dough onto your prepared baking sheet, spacing them about 2 inches (5 cm) apart. Press a few additional chocolate chunks into the top of each cookie, if desired.

Bake the cookies for 8–10 minutes, until the edges have set. They'll look a little soft and underbaked at first, but they'll continue to firm up as they cool. Allow the cookies to cool on the baking sheet for about 10 minutes before transferring them to a wire rack to cool completely. As soon as they've cooled, cover them tightly and store them at room temperature for up to 7 days.

NOTES

For best results, use a store-bought, no-stir variety of almond butter because the natural oils could alter the texture.

Cornstarch will also work in place of the arrowroot powder.

Chunky Monkey Oatmeal Cookies

GLUTEN-FREE, OIL-FREE, DAIRY-FREE OPTION*

Like the Chunky Monkey Muffins (page 74), these healthy cookies are loaded with sweet bananas, rich dark chocolate and crunchy nuts. But while the muffins are light and fluffy, their cookie counterparts are extra chewy and soft. If you ever find yourself in a position where you're craving something but you don't know exactly what, I'm willing to bet that these cookies will satisfy that craving.

YIELD: 18-22 COOKIES

½ cup (128 g) almond butter

1 large egg

1 medium-sized ripe banana, mashed (about ½ cup [100 g])

⅓ cup (78 ml) maple syrup

1 tsp vanilla extract

1 tsp baking soda

1 tbsp (7 g) arrowroot powder

1½ cups (121 g) old-fashioned rolled oats

½ cup (58 g) walnuts or pecans, coarsely chopped

½ cup (90 g) coarsely chopped dark chocolate chunks (*for dairy-free, use vegan dark chocolate)

Preheat your oven to 350°F (177°C) and line a cookie sheet with parchment paper or a non-stick baking mat. Set aside.

In a large mixing bowl, use an electric mixer to beat the almond butter, egg, banana, maple syrup and vanilla for about 1-2 minutes or until the mixture becomes smooth and creamy. Add the baking soda and arrowroot powder, and continue beating for about 30 seconds or until both dry ingredients become well incorporated. Finally, fold in the oats, nuts and chocolate chunks by hand.

Using a rounded tablespoon, drop the dough onto your prepared baking sheet, spacing them about 2 inches (5 cm) apart.

Bake the cookies for 10-12 minutes, until the edges begin to turn golden brown. They'll seem a little soft and underbaked at first, but they'll continue to firm up as they cool. Allow the cookies to cool on the baking sheet for about 10 minutes before transferring them to a wire rack to cool completely. As soon as they've cooled, cover them tightly and store them at room temperature for up to 7 days.

NOTES

For best results, use a store-bought, no-stir variety of almond butter because the natural oils could alter the texture.

Cornstarch will also work in place of the arrowroot powder.

Pumpkin Spice Cookies

GLUTEN-FREE, GRAIN-FREE, OIL-FREE, DAIRY-FREE

You would never believe that a combination of such simple, grain-free ingredients could produce a cookie that's so big on taste. Subtly sweet with just the perfect amount of spice, these soft and chewy cookies are perfect for those who love the warm and comforting flavors of fall. For an extra special treat, add ½ cup (90 g) of dark chocolate chips to the dough right before baking.

YIELD: 18-22 COOKIES

¾ cup (192 g) almond butter

1 large egg

¼ cup (58 g) canned pumpkin puree

½ cup (100 g) coconut palm sugar

1 tsp vanilla extract

2 tsp (5 g) ground cinnamon

1 tsp ground ginger

½ tsp ground nutmeg

1 tbsp (7 g) arrowroot powder

½ tsp baking soda

Preheat your oven to 350°F (177°C) and line a cookie sheet with parchment paper or a non-stick baking mat. Set aside.

In a large mixing bowl, use an electric mixer to beat the almond butter, egg, pumpkin, coconut palm sugar, vanilla, cinnamon, ginger and nutmeg for about 1-2 minutes or until the mixture becomes smooth and creamy. Add the arrowroot powder and baking soda, and continue beating for about 30 seconds or until both dry ingredients become well incorporated.

Using a rounded tablespoon, drop the dough onto your prepared baking sheet, spacing them about 2 inches (5 cm) apart. The dough will feel a little on the thinner side, but this is completely normal. Just do your best to give it a circular shape and smooth out the tops with the back of the spoon.

Bake the cookies for 12-14 minutes, until the edges begin to turn golden brown. They'll seem a little soft and underbaked at first, but they'll continue to firm up as they cool. Allow the cookies to cool on the baking sheet for about 10 minutes before transferring them to a wire rack to cool completely. These cookies change texture based on how you store them, so keep them in a sealed container for a softer texture or leave them uncovered on the counter for a slightly firmer one.

NOTES

For best results, use a store-bought, no-stir variety of almond butter because the natural oils could alter the texture.

You could also use brown sugar instead of the coconut palm sugar.

Cornstarch will also work in place of the arrowroot powder.

Apple Cinnamon Oatmeal Cookies

GLUTEN-FREE, OIL-FREE, DAIRY-FREE

I spent quite a bit of time fighting with these cookies before finally perfecting them, but I was determined to make them work because of how delicious they tasted even when the texture wasn't quite there. It just goes to show that persistence pays off, because these subtly sweet, spiced apple cookies turned out to be some of my favorites. The only thing I'd advise is to store them uncovered since they tend to get extra soft when sealed.

YIELD: 16-20 COOKIES

¾ cup (192 g) almond butter

1 large egg

6 tbsp (75 g) coconut palm sugar

¼ cup (59 ml) unsweetened applesauce

1 tsp vanilla extract

2 tsp (5 g) ground cinnamon

1 tsp baking soda

1¾ cups (141 g) old-fashioned rolled oats

1 cup (120 g) finely diced apple (about 1 medium apple)

Preheat your oven to 350°F (177°C) and line a cookie sheet with parchment paper or a non-stick baking mat. Set aside.

In a large mixing bowl, use an electric mixer to beat the almond butter, egg, coconut palm sugar, applesauce and vanilla for about 1-2 minutes or until the mixture becomes smooth and creamy. Add the cinnamon and baking soda, and continue beating for about 30 seconds or until both become well incorporated. Finally, fold in the oats and diced apple by hand.

Using a heaping tablespoon, drop the dough onto your prepared baking sheet, spacing them about 2 inches (5 cm) apart. The dough might seem a bit wet, but this is normal.

Bake the cookies for 13-15 minutes, until the edges begin to turn golden brown. They'll seem a little soft and underbaked at first, but they'll continue to firm up as they cool. Allow the cookies to cool on the baking sheet for about 15 minutes before transferring them to a wire rack to cool completely. As soon as they've cooled, cover them tightly and store them at room temperature for up to 7 days.

NOTES

For best results, use a store-bought, no-stir variety of almond butter because the natural oils could alter the texture.

You could also use brown sugar in place of the coconut palm sugar.

Banana Oat Breakfast Cookies

GLUTEN−FREE, VEGAN, REFINED SUGAR−FREE OPTION*

Sweetened with bananas, applesauce and a touch of honey and jam, these hearty little oatmeal cookies are proof that you can feel good about eating dessert for breakfast. Switch up the type of jam you use to give these cookies a totally new flavor, or leave out the jam and add ½ cup (90 g) of chocolate chips. Or you could use raisins or nuts instead of the chocolate chips!

YIELD: 12−14 COOKIES

1 medium-sized ripe banana, mashed (about ½ cup [100 g])

½ cup (118 ml) unsweetened applesauce

¼ cup (60 ml) maple syrup

2 tbsp (30 ml) coconut oil, melted

2 tbsp (14 g) ground flaxseed

1 tsp baking powder

1 tsp vanilla extract

1½ cups (121 g) old-fashioned rolled oats

½ cup (60 g) oat bran

2–3 tbsp (30–45 ml) of your favorite jam (*for refined sugar–free, use a jam that's sweetened with fruit juice)

Preheat your oven to 350°F (177°C) and line a cookie sheet with parchment paper or a non-stick baking mat. Set aside.

Mash the banana in a large mixing bowl. Add all the remaining ingredients except for the oats, oat bran and jam, and mix until well combined. Finally, stir in the oats and oat bran.

Using a rounded tablespoon, drop the dough onto your prepared baking sheet, spacing them about 2 inches (5 cm) apart. Use your fingers to shape the cookies (they won't change much in the oven), and use your thumb or the back of a ½ teaspoon measuring spoon to make an indentation in the top of each cookie. Fill that indentation up with ½ teaspoon of jam.

Bake the cookies for 12–14 minutes, until the edges begin to turn golden brown. They'll seem a little soft and underbaked at first, but they'll continue to firm up as they cool. Allow the cookies to cool on the baking sheet for about 10 minutes before transferring them to a wire rack to cool completely. As soon as they've cooled, cover them tightly and store them at room temperature for up to 5 days.

White Chocolate Macadamia Cookies

GLUTEN-FREE, GRAIN-FREE, OIL-FREE

While it's not technically chocolate due to a lack of cocoa, it doesn't change the fact that white chocolate is a perfect partner for macadamia nuts. For an even bigger treat for your taste buds, use macadamia nuts that are roasted and lightly salted. The sweet and salty combo is to die for.

YIELD: 18–22 COOKIES

1 cup (256 g) almond butter

1 large egg

6 tbsp (89 ml) maple syrup

1 tsp vanilla extract

2 tbsp (14 g) coconut flour

1 tbsp (7 g) arrowroot powder

1 tsp baking soda

½ cup (90 g) white chocolate chips

½ cup (50 g) macadamia nuts, chopped

Preheat your oven to 350°F (177°C) and line a cookie sheet with parchment paper or a non-stick baking mat. Set aside.

In a large mixing bowl, use an electric mixer to beat the almond butter, egg, maple syrup and vanilla for about 1–2 minutes or until the mixture becomes smooth and creamy. Add the coconut flour, arrowroot powder and baking soda, and continue beating until all the dry ingredients become well incorporated. Finally, fold in the chocolate and nuts by hand.

Using a rounded tablespoon, drop the dough onto your prepared baking sheet, spacing them about 2 inches (5 cm) apart. Use a paper towel to gently press down on all the cookies to flatten them slightly—this will absorb some of the excess oil from the almond butter and will help shape them. Press a few additional chocolate chips and nuts into the tops of the cookies, if desired.

Bake the cookies for 7–9 minutes, until the edges begin to turn golden brown. They'll look a little soft and underbaked at first, but they'll continue to firm up as they cool. Allow the cookies to cool on the baking sheet for about 10 minutes before transferring them to a wire rack to cool completely. As soon as they've cooled, cover them tightly and store them at room temperature for up to 7 days.

NOTES

For these cookies, I recommend using almond butter for its milder taste. You could use peanut butter, but the flavor will shine through. For best results, use a store-bought, no-stir variety because the natural oils could alter the texture.

Cornstarch will also work in place of the arrowroot powder.

Chewy Ginger Molasses Cookies

GLUTEN-FREE, GRAIN-FREE, OIL-FREE, DAIRY-FREE

It doesn't have to be Christmas for you to enjoy these soft and chewy gingerbread-like cookies!
Loaded with warming spices and a rich molasses taste, they have that old-fashioned appeal that both adults
and kids will enjoy. The outsides are extra crunchy thanks to large crystals of turbinado cane sugar,
while the insides remain soft, chewy and absolutely irresistible.

YIELD: 16–20 COOKIES

1 cup (256 g) almond butter

1 large egg

¼ cup (88 g) molasses

2 tbsp (43 g) honey

1 tbsp (7 g) arrowroot powder

1 tsp baking soda

1 tsp ground cinnamon

½ tsp ground ginger

¼ tsp ground cloves

¼ tsp ground nutmeg

Turbinado cane sugar, for sprinkling

Preheat your oven to 350°F (177°C) and line a cookie sheet with parchment paper or a non-stick baking mat. Set aside.

In a large mixing bowl, use an electric mixer to beat the almond butter, egg, molasses and honey for about 1–2 minutes or until the mixture becomes smooth and creamy. Add the arrowroot powder, baking soda, cinnamon, ginger, cloves and nutmeg, and continue beating for about 30 seconds or until all the dry ingredients become well incorporated.

Use a rounded tablespoon to scoop out the dough and roll it into a ball between your hands. Drop the dough onto your prepared baking sheet, spacing them about 2 inches (5 cm) apart. Liberally sprinkle the tops with cane sugar, pressing the crystals in slightly.

Bake the cookies for 10–12 minutes. Allow them to cool on the baking sheet for about 10 minutes before transferring them to a wire rack to cool completely. As soon as they've cooled, cover them tightly and store them at room temperature for up to 7 days.

NOTES

For best results, use a store-bought, no-stir variety of almond butter because the natural oils could alter the texture.

Cornstarch will also work in place of the arrowroot powder.

You could also use regular granulated sugar for sprinkling.

Honey Almond Oatmeal Cookies

GLUTEN-FREE, DAIRY-FREE, REFINED SUGAR-FREE

I went through a really long phase where honey, almonds and oats were my absolute favorite baking staples. And if I'm being honest, they're still the ingredients I turn to the most. Delicious on their own, they come together to create a combination that's both healthy and impossible to resist—kind of like these soft and chewy cookies.

YIELD: 14 COOKIES

½ cup (128 g) almond butter

1 large egg

¼ cup (85 g) honey

2 tbsp (30 ml) melted coconut oil

½ tsp almond extract

¼ cup (24 g) almond flour

1 tbsp (7 g) arrowroot powder

1 tsp baking soda

1 cup (80 g) old-fashioned rolled oats

½ cup (50 g) sliced blanched almonds

Preheat your oven to 350°F (177°C) and line a cookie sheet with parchment paper or a non-stick baking mat. Set aside.

In a large mixing bowl, use an electric mixer to beat the almond butter, egg, honey, coconut oil and almond extract for about 1–2 minutes or until the mixture becomes smooth and creamy. Add the almond flour, arrowroot powder and baking soda, and continue beating for about 30 seconds or until each becomes well incorporated. Finally, stir in the oats and sliced almonds by hand.

Using a rounded tablespoon, drop the dough onto your prepared baking sheet, spacing about 2 inches (5 cm) apart.

Bake the cookies for 8–10 minutes, until the edges begin to turn golden brown. They'll seem a little soft and underbaked at first, but they'll continue to firm up as they cool. Allow the cookies to cool on the baking sheet for about 10 minutes before transferring them to a wire rack to cool completely. As soon as they've cooled, cover them tightly and store them at room temperature for up to 7 days.

NOTES

For best results, use a store-bought, no-stir variety of almond butter because the natural oils could alter the texture.

Cornstarch will also work in place of the arrowroot powder.

Dark Chocolate Coconut Cookies

GLUTEN-FREE, GRAIN-FREE, OIL-FREE, DAIRY-FREE OPTION*

Like the No-Bake Dark Chocolate Coconut Granola Bars (page 141), these soft and chewy cookies feature an irresistible combination of chocolate, coconut and nut butter that makes them disappear fast. I used almond butter because of my allergies, but I hear they're pretty amazing with peanut butter, too!

YIELD: 12 COOKIES

½ cup (128 g) almond butter

1 large egg

⅓ cup (78 ml) maple syrup

1 tsp vanilla extract

1 tbsp (7 g) arrowroot powder

1 tsp baking soda

1 cup (90 g) unsweetened coconut, flaked or shredded

⅓ cup (59 g) coarsely chopped dark chocolate (*for dairy-free, use vegan dark chocolate)

Preheat your oven to 350°F (177°C) and line a cookie sheet with parchment paper or a non-stick baking mat. Set aside.

In a large mixing bowl, use an electric mixer to beat the almond butter, egg, maple syrup and vanilla for about 1–2 minutes or until the mixture becomes smooth and creamy. Add the arrowroot powder and baking soda, and continue beating until both dry ingredients become well incorporated. Finally, fold in the coconut and chocolate chunks by hand.

Using a rounded tablespoon, drop the dough onto your prepared baking sheet, spacing about 2 inches (5 cm) apart. Press a few additional chocolate chunks into the tops of the cookies, if desired.

Bake the cookies for 10–12 minutes, until the edges begin to turn golden brown. They'll look a little soft and underbaked at first, but they'll continue to firm up as they cool. Allow the cookies to cool on the baking sheet for about 10 minutes before transferring them to a wire rack to cool completely. As soon as they've cooled, cover them tightly and store them at room temperature for up to 7 days.

NOTES

For best results, use a store-bought, no-stir variety of almond butter because the natural oils could alter the texture.

Cornstarch will also work in place of the arrowroot powder.

Baking the Perfect Muffin

I know how frustrating it can be to go into a recipe with high hopes and have it turn out nothing like you were expecting, and because I can't hang out in your kitchen and make muffins with you, I wanted to include some tips and tricks I picked up along the way that'll help you bake up a perfect batch every time.

THE BLENDER

Almost all of the muffin recipes in this book call for a high-speed blender to do the mixing, as it's the best way to ensure that the oats (which act as the "flour") break down finely enough to make muffins that are light and fluffy. If your oats don't break down well enough, your muffins will come out denser and flatter, and you'll be able to feel small oat pieces in the finished product. That's not necessarily a bad thing, but if you want a smooth texture that's most like a traditional muffin, a high-speed blender is the way to go.

That being said, I know high-speed blenders like the Vitamix (what I used) or Blendtec tend to be a bit of an investment, which is why I suggest two alternative methods that work almost as well:

A FOOD PROCESSOR

This operates on the same basic idea, so simply swap out the blender in the instructions for a food processor—just make sure that you're running it for long enough and scraping down the sides so that no bigger oat chunks remain and the batter is smooth and creamy. I tested out both a higher power food processor and a more basic run-of-the-mill processor and both worked, but I found that the basic one did leave slightly larger oat pieces.

YOUR HANDS

While you can't technically break down oats with your hands, you can use pre-ground oat flour and mix all the ingredients by hand in a big bowl, following the same steps of the recipe. You can also use a regular blender or food processor to do the mixing and simply replace the oats with oat flour if you're worried about its ability to break down the oats.

Here's a helpful chart for converting the oat measurements in the recipes to oat flour:

¾ cup (60 g) oats = ½ cup + 1 tbsp (60 g) oat flour

1 cup (80 g) oats = ¾ cup (80 g) oat flour

1¼ cup (101 g) oats = ¾ + 2 tbsp (101 g) oat flour

1½ cup (121 g) oats = 1 cup + 1 tbsp (121 g) oat flour

1¾ cup (141 g) oats = 1¼ cup (141 g) oat flour

2 cups (161 g) oats = 1½ cup (161 g) oat flour

A KITCHEN SCALE

While all of the recipes in this book include both cup and gram measurements, I strongly recommend investing in a simple food scale if you want the most consistent and accurate results. Not only does it ensure that you don't incorrectly measure out dry ingredients by over- or under-packing measuring cups that can vary in size by manufacturer, but it saves a lot of time and cleanup when measuring out wet ingredients like almond butter or honey because you simply put the blender container right on the food scale and scoop or pour them in!

THE NUT BUTTER

Almost all of the recipes in this book call for almond butter, and I tested them using Barney Butter Smooth Almond Butter. I like using almond butter because it has a milder flavor than something like peanut butter, so it doesn't get in the way of the recipe's other flavors. That being said, you could easily use cashew or peanut butter if you don't mind the flavor shining through a little. The only thing I'd suggest is to use a store-bought nut butter that doesn't require any stirring, as the natural oils could alter the texture of the finished product. I did test out natural almond butters as well, and while they still worked, I don't feel comfortable recommending them because of the inconsistency in texture between a new jar (runnier) and an older jar (drier).

NUT ALLERGY SUBSTITUTIONS

As someone who suffers from an allergy to peanuts, I know how annoying it can be to not be able to make a recipe just because of your allergies. While the recipes in this book rely heavily on almond butter, you can easily swap that out with a roasted soy nut butter to achieve the same results. There's a particular brand called Wowbutter that I swear by, as it has an ideal texture and is 100 percent nut-free. I would avoid using a sunflower seed butter, as it will react with baking soda to turn your muffins green. In addition to using a soy nut butter, you'll also have to replace the almond milk with another non-dairy milk like rice or soy.

THE OATS

Oats are another key player in almost all of the recipes in this book. They act as the "flour" for the muffins, and help make them deliciously light and fluffy. You can use either quick oats or old-fashioned oats in most of the recipes unless otherwise specified, but I wouldn't recommend using steel cut since they're much harder to break down. And while oats are naturally gluten-free, there's a chance for them to become contaminated during processing, so make sure to use certified gluten-free oats if you need your muffins to be gluten-free.

THE CHOCOLATE CHIPS

While you can easily use any chocolate chips you have on hand, I prefer using mini chips since they're not as heavy and there's less of a chance for them to sink to the bottom of the muffins during baking. If you're looking for good dairy-free chocolate chips, I recommend the Enjoy Life brand.

THE MUFFIN LINERS

I used standard muffin pans for all of these recipes, and in almost all cases, parchment paper muffin liners. I prefer these instead of regular paper muffin liners because there's almost no chance for them to stick and ruin the muffin. My second choice would be to grease the muffin pan really well, but I still prefer using liners because: there's less to clean; there's less of a chance for the outside of the muffin to burn; and the muffins come out neatly wrapped up and ready to go.

And that's that! Flourless baking can seem a little intimidating when you're just starting out, but I promise you that it's super simple . . . especially the more you do it! Does that mean I think you should practice by making every recipe in this book? You betcha!

Acknowledgments

Before I started working on this project, I had absolutely no idea how much work went into a cookbook, and I know for a fact there's no way I would have been able to do this alone.

Thank you so much to my editor, Sarah Monroe, who saw enough potential in me after stumbling across my blog to reach out and offer me a chance to bring to reality something that I previously only dreamed about. Your guidance helped me make this book the best that I possibly could. And thank you to the entire team at Page Street Publishing who transformed the initial vision into the book you're currently holding in your hands. You were an absolute joy to work with.

Thank you to my family and friends who supported me every step of the way and were my #1 cheerleaders through it all. Thank you, Mom, for never being too busy to bake chocolate chip oatmeal cookies with me when I was little. You're the reason I love healthy baking as much as I do, and I wouldn't have been able to make all these recipes without you. I'll remember our times in the kitchen, always. And thank you, Dad, for believing in me enough to buy me my first "big girl" camera and tell me to chase my dreams. You knew I had it in me even when I didn't, and I promise to always "add more chocolate." Just for you.

And last but definitely not least, thank you to all my amazing readers and to anyone who's ever made my recipes. Your support is the reason I'm sitting here writing the acknowledgments in my very first cookbook, and don't think for a moment that I'll ever forget it. You guys rock my socks off.

About the Author

Amanda Drozdz is the health coach, recipe developer and food photographer behind the blog Running with Spoons. After graduating with a degree in psychology, she discovered a passion for using food to help people look and feel their best, and her own sweet tooth motivated her to create healthy snacks and desserts that can be enjoyed on a daily basis. She's worked with companies like Silk, Udi's Gluten Free and Blendtec, and her recipes have been featured on the websites of *Shape*, *Women's Health* and *Fitness*. She's an avid snowboarder, car enthusiast and lives her own version of healthy with a cookie in one hand and a carrot in the other.

www.runningwithspoons.com

www.facebook.com/RunningWithSpoons

twitter.com/RunWithSpoons

www.pinterest.com/runwithspoons

Index